The Official Strategy Guide

Brian Boyle

Prima Publishing
Rocklin, California
(916) 632-4400
www.primagames.com

Important:

Prima Publishing has made every effort to determine that the information contained in this book is accurate. However, the publisher makes no warranty, either expressed or implied, as to the accuracy, effectiveness, or completeness of the material in this book; nor does the publisher assume liability for damages, either incidental or consequential, that may result from using the information in this book. The publisher cannot provide information regarding game play, hints and strategies, or problems with hardware or software. Questions should be directed to the support numbers provided by the game and device manufacturers in their documentation. Some game tricks require precise timing and may require repeated attempts before the desired result is achieved.

ISBN: 7615-1239-X
Library of Congress Catalog Card Number: 97-069034
Printed in the United States of America

97 98 99 00 GG 10 9 8 7 6 5 4 3 2 1

Acknowledgments

"There Is No 'i' In 'Team'"

My deepest, most sincere, most *humble* thanks to the extended family of Team Prima:

Brooke Raymond, my project editor

Amy Raynor, my acquisitions editor

Sam Mills, my copy editor

Jeremy Conrad, my tech editor

Cathi Marsh, for her design and layout

Friends, without you, I am nothing.

Also thanks to Kirk Somdal and Sanders Keel at THQ.

Brian Boyle

October 9, 1997

Brian Boyle is a technical editor and software reviewer, as well as the author of *Dark Earth: The Official Strategy Guide* and co-author of *Interstate '76™: The Official Strategy Guide,* also available from Prima.

Table of Contents

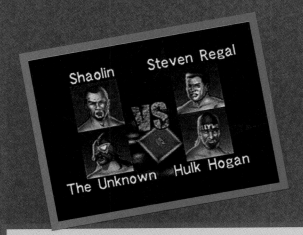

PART ONE

Game Power

Step Into the Squared Circle—
It's Time to Dance!

Ask yourself, do you want to be a face[1] or a green[2] heel[3]? Do you want your card[4] to be filled with duds[5] or squashes[6]? Do you want to be the draw[7] that fills the house[8]? With *WCW vs. NWO: World Tour—The Official Strategy Guide* to show you the way, your house will pop[9] with heat[10] and your finishes[11] will be pumped with spots[12]. *WCW vs. NWO: World Tour—The Official Strategy Guide* is no kayfabe[13]; you won't need a save[14] with this book at your side! Don't blow up[15]. Turn every dance[16] into a shoot[17], stretch[18] your opponents, and maybe even draw a little hardway juice[19]. You've got *WCW vs. NWO: World Tour—The Official Strategy Guide* in your corner!

[1] a good guy

[2] inexperienced

[3] a bad guy

[4] the matches scheduled for the same day in the same arena

[5] a dull match

[6] a match where one wrestler totally dominates his opponent

[7] a popular wrestler

[8] the fans in attendance at the card

[9] unexpected heat (see [10])

[10] big excitement from the house

[11] the conclusion of a match

[12] the unforgettable highlights of a match

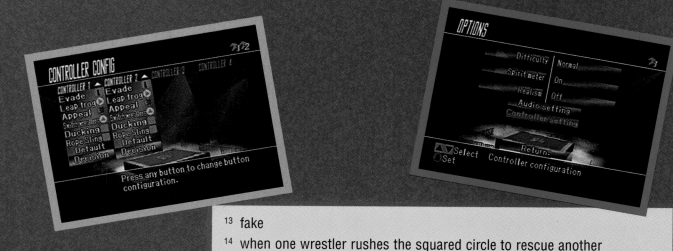

13 fake

14 when one wrestler rushes the squared circle to rescue another wrestler from a beating

15 weary, drained of strength

16 a match

17 real action with real injuries; not a kayfabe

18 when a wrestler squashes his opponent without hurting him

19 blood, when drawn unexpectedly—the "hard way"

Game Controls—Controller Setting

Your Nintendo® 64 controller is fully customizable, and you may alter the default settings to fit your own personal style. Also note that if you want to, you may assign a function such as Ducking to an entirely separate button.

So—What Do They Do?

Here's what the Nintendo 64's controller buttons actually control.

Control Stick: Taunt your opponent. Appeal to the crowd. Special Attack (+ Grapple, Long, when your Spirit Meter flashes "Special!").

Control Pad: Move your wrestler around the ring.

Start: Pauses the game.

C Button Down (▼): Run in the direction you're facing. Go for the pin when your opponent is on the mat.

C Button Left/Right (◄ ►): Change your wrestler's costume when you're selecting a wrestler.

A Button, Tap Ⓐ: Grapple, Weak. Accept and advance in the menu screens.

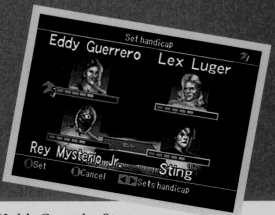

A Button, Press and Hold: Grapple, Strong.

B Button, Tap Ⓑ: Attack, Weak. Hit your opponent with a foreign object. Cancel and return to the previous menu screen.

B Button, Press and Hold Ⓑ: Attack, Strong.

L Button (Ⓛ): Avoid a grapple. Change the wrestling organization when you're selecting a wrestler.

C Button Up (▲): Flip a fallen or standing opponent. Snatch a foreign object from the crowd when you're outside the ring. Climb up out of the ring (+ D Pad).

C Button Right (▶): Switch your wrestler's attention to a different opponent in Battle Royale, Handicap, and Tag Team modes.

C Button Down (▼): Climb up onto the turnbuckle (+ D Pad). Run.

R Button (Ⓡ): Block. Reverse. Change the wrestling organization when you're selecting a wrestler.

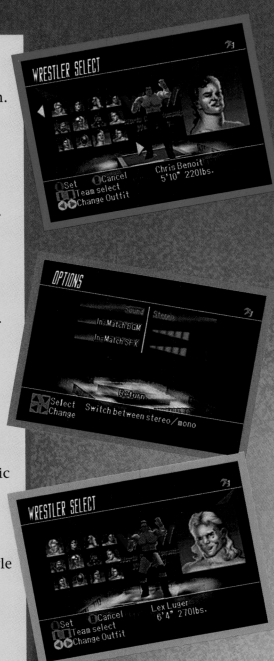

Game Controls—Audio Setting

Alter the Audio settings to your liking. You may choose from mono or stereo, and set sound levels for the background music and sound effects.

Game Controls—Option

You may change a number of options to suit your playing style and skill level.

Difficulty: Easy, Normal, or Hard.

Spirit Meter: Reflects the level of adrenaline and emotion the wrestler fights with. When the Spirit Meter is full, and begins to flash "Special!," the wrestler may execute his Special Move or Blow.

Realism: If you select Realism On, the wrestlers will display the injuries they've accumulated over the course of the match.

The Basics—Moves and Holds

A nice feature of *WCW vs. NWO: World Tour* is that there are no insanely complicated, impossible-to-execute button combos to memorize. Each wrestler fights using the same basic button combinations, with very few exceptions (not all wrestlers have all types of moves).

In other words, even though the move or the hold your wrestler *actually* pulls off varies widely from wrestler to wrestler (depending on that wrestler's fighting style), the *type* of move or hold it is, and the button combination for executing it, remain the same for all 43 wrestlers, including the six bosses.

You determine how strong each attack or grapple will be—Weak or Strong—by the length of time you press and hold the Ⓑ or Ⓐ buttons, respectively. Within each *type* of attack or grapple, there are four different moves, depending on not only the length of time you press the button (obviously), but on your distance from your opponent.

Making It Happen

Part Two, "The Wrestlers," contains the complete list of moves and holds for each wrestler. The appendix, "The Bosses," reveals all the button commands for *WCW vs. NWO: World Tour*'s hidden characters. Here are a few basics:

- Grapple, Weak: Tap the Ⓐ button.
- Grapple, Strong: Press and hold the Ⓐ button.
- Post: While your opponent is on the mat, move to the nearest turnbuckle and press the Ⓑ button. Note: Opponent might have to be square with mat for signature move.
- Post: While your opponent is standing, move to the nearest turnbuckle and press the Ⓑ button.

- Rope Dive: Run toward the ropes you're facing by pressing the ▼ button. On the rebound, press and hold the Ⓐ button.
- Turnbuckle Jump: Move to the nearest turnbuckle and press the ▼ button.

Basic Game Power: Holds

Your wrestler has several holds that will differ depending on how near or far you are from your opponent, and how long you press the Ⓐ button. If you grapple your opponent from far away and press the Ⓐ button for a short time, you'll execute a "weak" hold, such as a Punch to Face. If you grapple your opponent from up close and press the Ⓐ button for a long time, you execute a "strong" hold, such as a Power Lift Body Slam.

Winning is all about timing. One way to practice timing your moves is to plug a second controller into your Nintendo 64, and set Player Two for human control (not the CPU). The second wrestler will just stand there, letting you pummel him mercilessly, while you perfect your technique and your timing.

Basic Game Power: Blows

Your wrestler has several blows that will vary depending on how close or distant you are from your opponent, and how long you hold down the Ⓑ button. If you attack your opponent from a distance and tap the Ⓑ button quickly, you execute a "weak" punching attack, such as a Slap Chest. Attack your opponent from nearby and hold the Ⓑ button for a long time, and you execute a "strong" kicking attack, such as a Knee Kick.

If you've dropped your opponent to the mat, you can then execute either a Blow Attack or a Joint Attack. Blow Attacks are moves such as elbow drops, standing flips, stomps, and so on. Joint Attacks are striking moves and submission holds. For example, if you're standing over your opponent's legs and you press the Ⓐ button, you might pull off a Camel Clutch. If you're standing over your opponent's legs and you press the Ⓐ button, you might also pull off a Groin Sever Spread.

Watch your opponent's Spirit Meter very closely. As you pummel your opponent, or wrap him up in a Submission Hold, his Spirit will decrease. When his Spirit is almost gone, or you see his Spirit Meter flash the "Danger!" message, you can put him away once and for all!

Basic Game Power: Counters

If your opponent rushes you with a punching or kicking attack, your wrestler has a counter that you execute by pressing the Ⓡ button. Counter a punch with a move such as the One Arm Flip, or a kick with a move like the Standing Achilles. For added power, press the Ⓡ button and then the Ⓑ button for a counter with an extra attack.

Overpower an opponent's attack with the right move. A block move will overpower a punch or kick, a punching or kicking move will overpower a hold, and a hold move will overpower a block.

Basic Game Power: Special!

Each wrestler has a Special Blow that can't be countered. When you see your Spirit Meter flash the "Special!" message, you can execute your Special Blow by pressing and holding the Ⓐ button, and moving the Control Stick in any direction.

Even though your Special Blow can't be overpowered, don't use it too often or your opponent will know it's coming, and he'll be ready and waiting.

On the Apron

Ⓐ: Grapple with your opponent.

Ⓑ: Attack your opponent.

D Pad + ▼: Run.

D Pad (toward your opponent) + Ⓑ: Attack your opponent.

D Pad (toward the ring or floor) + ▲: Climb in or out of the ring.

D Pad (out of the ring) + Ⓐ: Flying Attack, outside the ring.

D Pad + Ⓑ: Leg Attack against an opponent on the apron.

Opponent Down

Ⓐ: Attack.

Ⓑ: Striking Attack.

Ⓡ: Pull your opponent to his feet.

▼: Pin your opponent.

Opponent Stunned

Grapple, Strong + Ⓡ (while you're behind your opponent): Lift your opponent up onto your shoulders.

Grapple, Strong + D Pad + Ⓐ or Ⓑ (if your opponent is cornered): Turnbuckle move.

Outside the Ring

D Pad (toward your opponent) + Ⓐ: Pull your opponent out of the ring.

D Pad (towards the ring) + ▲: Climb up onto the apron. Press it again to climb into the ring.

A Look Ahead

There are so many ways to play *WCW vs. NWO: World Tour*, you could spend literally months experiencing them all. To whet your appetite, here's a look ahead.

WCW vs. NWO

This is where the big boys of wrestling (World Championship Wrestling) go head-to-head with the bad boys of wrestling (New World Order).

WCW

Pick your team from the cream of WCW pro wrestling crop.

NWO

Coming on strong, NWO refuses to take a back seat to WCW. The wrestlers of NWO are here to stay—and they mean business!

Exhibition Match

Are you ready to rumble? Then prove you've got the draw: It's go time! Exhibition Match offers you a large variety of game-play options to choose from.

1 vs. 1 Single

What could be better than a little one-on-one to settle a score, teach a heel a lesson, or find out who's bad? 1 vs. 1 Single is a good way to go when you've got something to prove.

2 vs. 2 Tag

There's no better feeling than to hand some punk his head—except when a good buddy's by your side to laugh along with you! Some of the most exciting cards in wrestling consist of tag team dances.

1 vs. 2 Handicap

Are you the baddest wrestler this side of the Pacific? Are you the stiffest[20] worker[21] north of the border? Prove it! See how tough you are when you're wrestling all by yourself—against *two* opponents!

[20] Contact that causes injury, although usually not serious.

[21] A good wrestler who has a good workrate (the percentage of his good wrestling blows and holds to his bad or dull moves). Not to be confused with "work," which is fakery.

Battle Royale

Sometimes a little free-for-all grudge match is pro wrestling the way it ought to be—last man standing wins! Nothing could be more satisfying than that—as long as you're the last man!

League Challenge

Always a favorite event, League Challenge is the meat-and-potatoes of pro wrestling. If you defeat every wrestler in an individual organization, including your own, you'll face the hidden boss of that organization. Once you beat the boss, that wrestler may be saved to your Nintendo 64 Memory Pak. You may then pit that boss against other opponents, exactly the same as you would any of the other wrestlers featured in *WCW vs. NWO: World Tour*.

WCW

There is a Starrcade title match for each of the Single, Tag Team, and Cruiserweight divisions—so get ready to rock!

HEAVYWEIGHT CHAMPION

HEAVYWEIGHT TAG CHAMPION

CRUISERWEIGHT CHAMPION

NWO

NWO's Souled Out cards are the hottest paper[22] in pro wrestling! You can be a part of the action with a Souled Out title match for the Single and Tag Team divisions.

HEAVYWEIGHT CHAMPION

HEAVYWEIGHT TAG CHAMPION

[22] tickets

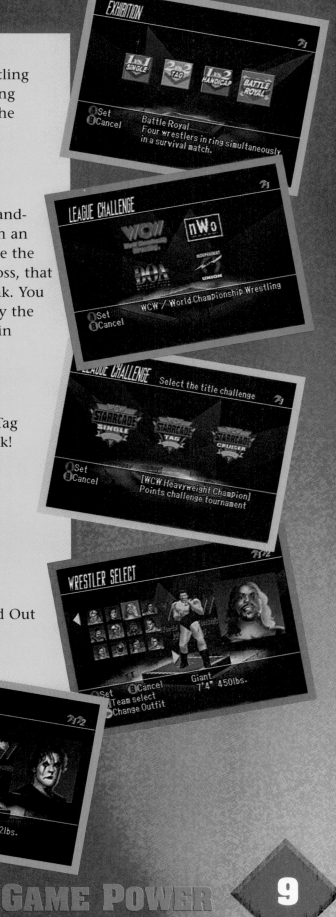

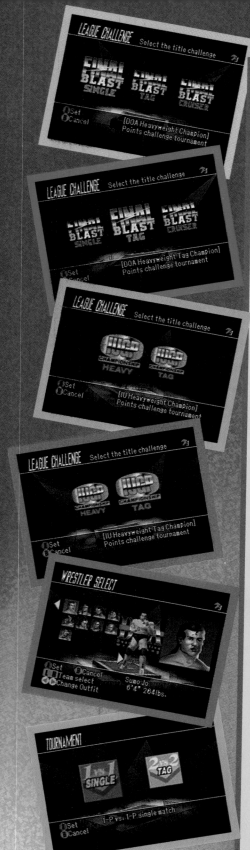

DOA

The outlaws of pro wrestling refuse to be left in the dust. They're here to stay, and they're thirsty for juice[23]! There's a Final Blast title match for each of the Single, Tag Team, and Cruiserweight divisions.

HEAVYWEIGHT CHAMPION

HEAVYWEIGHT TAG CHAMPION

CRUISERWEIGHT CHAMPION

Independent Union

You want to see clean jobs[24] and *real* action? Look no further than Independent Union Grand Prix title matches for the Single and Tag Team divisions.

HEAVYWEIGHT CHAMPION

HEAVYWEIGHT TAG CHAMPION

League

Possibly the purest form of pro wrestling, your individual league standing is determined by scoring three points per win, one point per draw, or zero points per loss in an up to 16-man (eight-team) round-robin tournament.

1 vs. 1 Single

2 vs. 2 Tag

Tournament

Taking the competition to a higher level, there's no "do over" for a green wrestler thrown out of this 16-man (eight-team) round-robin, single-elimination tournament.

1 vs. 1 Single

2 vs. 2 Tag

[23] blood
[24] A clean job is a loss without the use of prohibited moves.

Tips and Strategies

- Take advantage of a wrestler's weaknesses. Some wrestlers are more vulnerable to Punching and Kicking Attacks, while others are more vulnerable to Grapples.

- To determine if a wrestler is vulnerable to Attacks or Grapples, start each match by running to confront your opponent. Immediately unleash a string of Attacks. If your opponent throws out his chest to defy you, that wrestler is resistant to Attacks. Switch to Grapples immediately!

- Remember, though, you can pummel any wrestler, even those resistant to Attacks—*if* your Attacks are fast enough. Practice using the Ⓑ button—lay on a fast Attack, followed by strong Attack, followed by another fast Attack.

- Drain a wrestler's Spirit, even a wrestler with a flashing "Special," by striking him fast enough with Punching and Kicking Attacks. Use the shoulder buttons to avoid a Grapple!

- Combine attacks for maximum damage. Here's an example of how to use "combos":

1. Attack your opponent as fast as possible, without mercy, draining his Spirit.

2. Keep Attacking—back your opponent up against the ropes. Eventually, you'll knock him through the ropes onto the apron.

3. Wait for your opponent. When he stands up to climb back into the ring, grab him with a Grapple. Throw him back over the ropes into the ring.

4. Immediately move to his head or legs. Grab him in a Submission hold, draining more of his Spirit.

5. Wait for your opponent to stand. The second he gets on his feet, grab him in another Grapple. Throw him to the mat.

6. Immediately follow up with another Submission hold. Now he should be ready to pin!

This Is It—It's Time!

Get yourselves ready, wrestling fans: It's time to go to the dance!

PART TWO

The Wrestlers

Try these powerful moves out on your unsuspecting opponents:

- **Counter**   ®
- **Shoulder Charge**   ▼ + ®
- **Running Attack**   D Pad towards ropes + ▼ + ®

WCW

WCW (World Championship Wrestling) has a long history, with its roots in the original National Wrestling Alliance of 1948. The NWA held "Starrcade '83," the first wrestling supercard seen by more than 15,000 fans, in November 1983. A year later, Ric Flair won pro wrestling's first one million dollar prize when guest referee Smokin' Joe Frazier halted "Starrcade II": Flair's opponent, Dusty Rhodes, was bleeding too much.

In April 1987, the NWA purchased the UWF. Several UWF wrestlers, including Sting, joined the NWA. In November 1988, entrepreneur and media magnate Ted Turner bought the NWA. Turner's TBS "Superstation" featured the NWA's "World Championship Wrestling" TV program every Saturday night for several years. In December 1990, the National Wrestling Alliance was officially renamed World Championship Wrestling. Internationally celebrated wrestler Hulk Hogan joined WCW in June 1994.

Interestingly, since October 1990 ("Halloween Havoc '90") there have been several wrestlers who have pretended to be Sting for one reason or another, including Kevin Nash and the current fake "Sting" (a.k.a. "Stink"), the wrestler who used to be Cobra.

Lex Luger

LEX LUGER

Height: 6' 4"
Weight: 270 lbs.
Signature Move: Torture Rack

Profile

Lex Luger found wrestling stardom quickly after a standout gridiron career in the NFL, CFL, USFL, and with the University of Miami "Hurricanes." Luger cultivated this early fame using experienced, focused determination, and now stands unquestionably at the pinnacle of his career. Luger has been the backbone of WCW, combating NWO when other superstars scattered. Capable of "racking" the most behemoth opposition following a volley of devastating forearms, Luger has accumulated a distinguished record, including a WCW World Heavyweight championship, two WCW tag-team titles, and four WCW US belts.

Punching and Kicking Moves

Name of Move	Controller Command
Crown Chop	Tap Ⓑ close
Knee Kick	Tap Ⓑ far
Chest Slap	⇑ + Tap Ⓑ close
Mid Kick	⇑ + Tap Ⓑ far
Spinning Roundhouse	Hold Ⓑ
Drop Kick	⇑ + Hold Ⓑ

Front Grapples—Weak

Name of Move	Controller Command
Crown Bamboochop	Tap Ⓐ + Ⓐ
Super Elbow	Tap Ⓐ + ⇑ + Ⓐ
Body Slam	Tap Ⓐ + ⇓ + Ⓐ
Hiplock Takedown	Tap Ⓐ + Ⓑ
Skyscraper Backdrop	Tap Ⓐ + ⇑ + Ⓑ
Held Tombstone	Tap Ⓐ + ⇓ + Ⓑ

Rear Grapples—Weak

Name of Move	Controller Command
Backbone Shiver	Tap Ⓐ + Ⓐ
Shoulder Smash	Tap Ⓐ + Ⓑ

Front Grapples—Strong

Name of Move	Controller Command
Power Slam	Hold Ⓐ + Ⓐ
Bench Press Slam	Hold Ⓐ + ⇑ + Ⓐ
Manhattan Drop	Hold Ⓐ + ⇓ + Ⓐ
Standing Clothesline	Hold Ⓐ + Ⓑ
Dynamic DDT	Hold Ⓐ + ⇑ + Ⓑ
Dynamic Bomb	Hold Ⓐ + ⇓ + Ⓑ

Rear Grapples—Strong

Name of Move	Controller Command
Forearm Mickey	Hold Ⓐ + Ⓐ
Back Breaker	Hold Ⓐ + Ⓑ

Whip to Ropes

Name of Move	Controller Command
High Body Toss	Hold Ⓐ + D Pad toward ropes + ▼ + Tap Ⓐ
Arm-Drag Takedown	Hold Ⓐ + D Pad toward ropes + ▼ + ⇑ + Tap Ⓐ
Power Lift Body Slam	Hold Ⓐ + D Pad toward ropes + ▼ + Hold Ⓐ
Super Slam	Hold Ⓐ + D Pad toward ropes + ▼ + ⇑ + Hold Ⓐ

Special Attacks (When Spirit Meter Is Flashing)

FROM THE FRONT

Name of Move	Controller Command
Coconut Crush	Hold Ⓐ + Analog Stick

FROM THE REAR

Name of Move	Controller Command
Torture Rack	Hold Ⓐ + Analog Stick

Opponent on Mat

FACE UP

Name of Move	Controller Command
Arm Wrench	move near head, Tap Ⓐ
Knee Crush	move near legs, Tap Ⓐ
Elbow Drop	Tap Ⓑ

FACE DOWN

Name of Move	Controller Command
Camel Clutch	move near head, Tap Ⓐ
Boston Crab	move near legs, Tap Ⓐ
Stomp	Tap Ⓑ

Rope and Turnbuckle Moves

OPPONENT ON MAT

Name of Move	Controller Command
Flying Elbow	move into turnbuckle + ▼

OPPONENT STANDING

Name of Move	Controller Command
Diving Shoulder Block	move into turnbuckle + ▼

THROW GROGGY OPPONENT INTO TURNBUCKLE

Name of Move	Controller Command
Corner Crunch	Tap Ⓐ + Ⓐ
Aerial Brain Buster	Hold Ⓐ + Ⓐ
Diving Body Press	Hold Ⓐ + ⇑ + Ⓐ

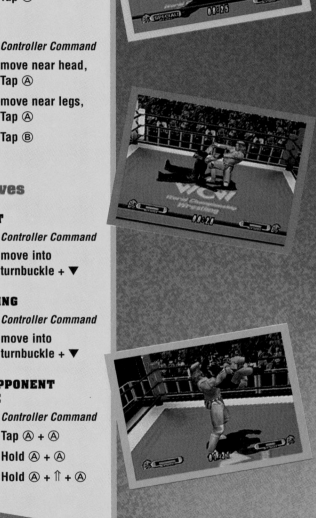

STING

Height: 6' 3"
Weight: 252 lbs.
Signature Move: Scorpion Death Lock

Profile

Shrouded in mystery and controversy, Sting lurks at the fringe of WCW vs. NWO battle lines. Draped in black and wielding a baseball bat, Sting has created a dark, silent aura that intimidates everyone. His allegiance only to himself has everyone guessing his next move. This native of Venice Beach, California, has been the "franchise" superstar of WCW since the promotion started.

Punching and Kicking Moves

Name of Move	Controller Command
Forearm Elbow	Tap Ⓑ close
Knee Kick	Tap Ⓑ far
Body Blow	⇑ + Tap Ⓑ close
Stomach Kick	⇑ + Tap Ⓑ far
Soccer Kick	Hold Ⓑ
Stinger Punch	⇑ + Hold Ⓑ

Front Grapples—Weak

Name of Move	Controller Command
1-Hand Hammer	Tap Ⓐ + Ⓐ
Shoulder Drop	Tap Ⓐ + ⇑ + Ⓐ
Body Slam	Tap Ⓐ + ⇓ + Ⓐ
Headlock Takedown	Tap Ⓐ + Ⓑ
Lifting Slam	Tap Ⓐ + ⇑ + Ⓑ
Back Buster	Tap Ⓐ + ⇓ + Ⓑ

Rear Grapples—Weak

Name of Move	Controller Command
Face Crusher	Tap Ⓐ + Ⓐ
Back Drop	Tap Ⓐ + Ⓑ

Front Grapples—Strong

Name of Move	Controller Command
Inside Side Buster	Hold Ⓐ + Ⓐ
Belly to Belly Suplex	Hold Ⓐ + ⇑ + Ⓐ
Power Bomb	Hold Ⓐ + ⇓ + Ⓐ
DDT	Hold Ⓐ + Ⓑ
Stinger Slam	Hold Ⓐ + ⇑ + Ⓑ
Small Package Press	Hold Ⓐ + ⇓ + Ⓑ

Rear Grapples—Strong

Name of Move	Controller Command
Scorpion Death Drop	Hold Ⓐ + Ⓐ
Atomic Slam	Hold Ⓐ + Ⓑ

Whip to Ropes

Name of Move	Controller Command
Arm-Drag Takedown	Hold Ⓐ + D Pad toward ropes + ▼ + Tap Ⓐ
Back Breaker Slam	Hold Ⓐ + D Pad toward ropes + ▼ + ⇑ + Tap Ⓐ
Press Slam	Hold Ⓐ + D Pad toward ropes + ▼ + Hold Ⓐ
Manhattan Drop	Hold Ⓐ + D Pad toward ropes + ▼ + ⇑ + Hold Ⓐ

Special Attacks (When Spirit Meter Is Flashing)

FROM THE FRONT

Name of Move	Controller Command
Power Jack	Hold Ⓐ + Analog Stick

FROM THE REAR

Name of Move	Controller Command
German Suplex	Hold Ⓐ + Analog Stick

Opponent on Mat

FACE UP

Name of Move	Controller Command
Sleeper Hold	move near head, Tap Ⓐ
Scorpion Death Lock	move near legs + Tap Ⓐ
Stomp	Tap Ⓑ

FACE DOWN

Name of Move	Controller Command
Camel Clutch	move near head, Tap Ⓐ
Leg Bar	move near legs, Tap Ⓐ
Smashing Blow	Tap Ⓑ

Rope and Turnbuckle Moves

OPPONENT ON MAT

Name of Move	Controller Command
Flying Knee	move into turnbuckle + ▼

OPPONENT STANDING

Name of Move	Controller Command
Diving Clothesline	move into turnbuckle + ▼

THROW GROGGY OPPONENT INTO TURNBUCKLE

Name of Move	Controller Command
Turnbuckle Slam	Tap Ⓐ + Ⓐ
Avalanche Suplex	Hold Ⓐ + ⇑ + Ⓐ
Super Brain Buster	Hold Ⓐ + Ⓐ
Stinger Splash	D pad toward turnbuckle + ▼ + Ⓑ

GIANT

Height: 7' 4"

Weight: 450 lbs.

Signature Moves: Choke Slam, Choke Hold

Profile

Destroying all in his path, the Giant has created tall tales, not fairy tales, with ferocious finality. Mammoth match-ending choke slams have gained awestruck attention for wrestling's "biggest" young superstar. The Giant, 25, grew quickly to become WCW's youngest world heavyweight champion by battling such renowned veterans as "Nature Boy" Ric Flair, Lex Luger, and "Macho Man" Randy Savage before surrendering the title to "Hollywood" Hulk Hogan. Recently adding to his growing accolades, the Giant prevailed at the three-ring, 60-man battle royal at *WCW World War 3* pay-per-view.

Punching and Kicking Moves

Name of Move	Controller Command
Clubbing Forearm	Tap Ⓑ close
Big Boot	Tap Ⓑ far
Ham Bone	⇑ + Tap Ⓑ close
Stomach Stuff	⇑ + Tap Ⓑ far
Head Kick	Hold Ⓑ
Super Kick	⇑ + Hold Ⓑ

Front Grapples—Weak

Name of Move	Controller Command
Head Butt	Tap Ⓐ + Ⓐ
Giant Forearm	Tap Ⓐ + ⇑ + Ⓐ
Body Slam	Tap Ⓐ + ⇓ + Ⓐ
Elbow Crank	Tap Ⓐ + Ⓑ
Standing Press Throw	Tap Ⓐ + ⇑ + Ⓑ
Neck Breaker	Tap Ⓐ + ⇓ + Ⓑ

Rear Grapples—Weak

Name of Move	Controller Command
Spine Tingler	Tap Ⓐ + Ⓐ
Knee Breaker	Tap Ⓐ + Ⓑ

Front Grapples—Strong

Name of Move	Controller Command
Top Rope Clothesline	Hold Ⓐ + Ⓐ
Canadian Back Breaker	Hold Ⓐ + ⇑ + Ⓐ
Double Arm Power Bomb	Hold Ⓐ + ⇓ + Ⓐ
Waist Sweep	Hold Ⓐ + Ⓑ
Choke Hold	Hold Ⓐ + ⇑ + Ⓑ
Pile Driver	Hold Ⓐ + ⇓ + Ⓑ

Rear Grapples—Strong

Name of Move	Controller Command
Inside Side Buster	Hold Ⓐ + Ⓐ
Giant Pain Rack	Hold Ⓐ + Ⓑ

Whip to Ropes

Name of Move	Controller Command
Overhead Toss	Hold Ⓐ + D Pad toward ropes + ▼ + Tap Ⓐ
Arm Bar Throw	Hold Ⓐ + D Pad toward ropes + ▼ + ⇑ + Tap Ⓐ
Power Slam	Hold Ⓐ + D Pad toward ropes + ▼ + Hold Ⓐ
Sleeper Hold	Hold Ⓐ + D Pad toward ropes + ▼ + ⇑ + Hold Ⓐ

Special Attacks (When Spirit Meter Is Flashing)

FROM THE FRONT

Name of Move	Controller Command
Choke Slam	Hold Ⓐ + Analog Stick

FROM THE REAR

Name of Move	Controller Command
Drop German Suplex	Hold Ⓐ + Analog Stick

Opponent on Mat

FACE UP

Name of Move	Controller Command
Choke	move near head, Tap Ⓐ
Leg Crush	move near legs, Tap Ⓐ
Falling Head Butt	Tap Ⓑ

FACE DOWN

Name of Move	Controller Command
Camel Clutch	move near head, Tap Ⓐ
Leg Screw	move near legs, Tap Ⓐ
Giant Leg Drop	Tap Ⓑ

Rope and Turnbuckle Moves

OPPONENT ON MAT

Name of Move	Controller Command
Giant Splash	move into turnbuckle + ▼

OPPONENT STANDING

Name of Move	Controller Command
Double Fist Drop	move into turnbuckle + ▼

THROW GROGGY OPPONENT INTO TURNBUCKLE

Name of Move	Controller Command
Turnbuckle Sandwich	Tap Ⓐ + Ⓐ
Giant Suplex	Hold Ⓐ + Ⓐ
Giant Swing Throw	Hold Ⓐ + ⇑ + Ⓐ
Giant Swing Throw	Hold Ⓐ + ⇑ + Ⓐ
Football Charge	D Pad toward turnbuckle + ▼ + Ⓑ

SCOTT STEINER

Height: 6' 1"

Weight: 235 lbs.

Signature Move: Belly to Back Suplex

Profile

Pulverized, tenderized—STEINERIZED! Scott Steiner, gifted with an eye-popping, Herculean physique, is always just a belly-to-belly suplex away from victory.

Punching and Kicking Moves

Name of Move	Controller Command
Elbow to Head	Tap Ⓑ close
Knee Kick	Tap Ⓑ far
Body Blow	⇑ + Tap Ⓑ close
Ricky Kick	⇑ + Tap Ⓑ far
Drop Kick	Hold Ⓑ
Linebacker Lift	⇑ + Hold Ⓑ

Front Grapples—Weak

Name of Move	Controller Command
Forearm Smash	Tap Ⓐ + Ⓐ
Fireman's Carry	Tap Ⓐ + ⇑ + Ⓐ
Shoulder Tackle	Tap Ⓐ + ⇓ + Ⓐ
Gut Wrench Suplex	Tap Ⓐ + Ⓑ
Snap Suplex	Tap Ⓐ + ⇑ + Ⓑ
Shoulder Breaker	Tap Ⓐ + ⇓ + Ⓑ

Rear Grapples—Weak

Name of Move	Controller Command
Back Breaker	Tap Ⓐ + Ⓐ
Throw German Suplex	Tap Ⓐ + Ⓑ

Front Grapples—Strong

Name of Move	Controller Command
Speedy Side Suplex	Hold Ⓐ + Ⓐ
Belly to Belly Suplex	Hold Ⓐ + ⇑ + Ⓐ
Stud Driver Bomb	Hold Ⓐ + ⇓ + Ⓐ
Front Suplex	Hold Ⓐ + Ⓑ
Belly to Back Suplex	Hold Ⓐ + ⇑ + Ⓑ
Screwdriver Power Slam	Hold Ⓐ + ⇓ + Ⓑ

Rear Grapples—Strong

Name of Move	Controller Command
Stretch Slam	Hold Ⓐ + Ⓐ
Full Nelson Suplex	Hold Ⓐ + Ⓑ

Whip to Ropes

Name of Move	Controller Command
Overhead Toss	Hold Ⓐ + D Pad toward ropes + ▼ + Tap Ⓐ
Full Press Slam	Hold Ⓐ + D Pad toward ropes + ▼ + ⇑ + Tap Ⓐ
Funky Steiner	Hold Ⓐ + D Pad toward ropes + ▼ + Hold Ⓐ
Frankensteiner Slam	Hold Ⓐ + D Pad toward ropes + ▼ + ⇑ + Hold Ⓐ

Special Attacks (When Spirit Meter Is Flashing)

FROM THE FRONT

Name of Move	Controller Command
Suplex Piledriver	Hold Ⓐ + Analog Stick

FROM THE REAR

Name of Move	Controller Command
Grapple Doctor Bomb	Hold Ⓐ + Analog Stick

Opponent on Mat

FACE UP

Name of Move	Controller Command
Dragon Sleeper	move near head, Tap Ⓐ
Boston Crab	move near legs, Tap Ⓐ
Elbow Drop	Tap Ⓑ

FACE DOWN

Name of Move	Controller Command
Camel Clutch	move near head, Tap Ⓐ
Knee Lock	move near legs, Tap Ⓐ
Falling Elbow	Tap Ⓑ

Rope and Turnbuckle Moves

OPPONENT ON MAT

Name of Move	Controller Command
Flying Elbow	move into turnbuckle + ▼

OPPONENT STANDING

Name of Move	Controller Command
Double Fist	move into turnbuckle + ▼
Turnbuckle Tackle	run toward ropes, ⇑ + Ⓐ

THROW GROGGY OPPONENT INTO TURNBUCKLE

Name of Move	Controller Command
Turnbuckle Tackle	Tap Ⓐ + Ⓐ
Avalanche Front Suplex	Hold Ⓐ + Ⓐ
Dragon Buster	Hold Ⓐ + ⇑ + Ⓐ

RICK STEINER

Height: 5' 11"

Weight: 248 lbs.

Signature Move: Canadian Backbreaker

Profile

Rick Steiner, known as the "Dog Face Gremlin," gives fans a spirited "woof, woof," while sporting his trademark coal black mustache, dog collar, and wrestling head gear. WCW tag teams now realize the super-size effect of being STEINERIZED!

Punching and Kicking Moves

Name of Move	Controller Command
Rough Elbow	Tap Ⓑ close
Knee Kick	Tap Ⓑ far
Hammer Punch	⇑ + Tap Ⓑ close
Soccer Kick	⇑ + Tap Ⓑ far
Shoulder Smash	Hold Ⓑ
Bulldog Forearm	⇑ + Hold Ⓑ

Front Grapples—Weak

Name of Move	Controller Command
Bull Elbow	Tap Ⓐ + Ⓐ
Bulldog Smash	Tap Ⓐ + ⇑ + Ⓐ
Lift Slam	Tap Ⓐ + ⇓ + Ⓐ
Head Lock Takedown	Tap Ⓐ + Ⓑ
Shoulder Press Slam	Tap Ⓐ + ⇑ + Ⓑ
Shoulder Buster	Tap Ⓐ + ⇓ + Ⓑ

Rear Grapples—Weak

Name of Move	Controller Command
Backbone Bull	Tap Ⓐ + Ⓐ
Overhead Slam	Tap Ⓐ + Ⓑ

Front Grapples—Strong

Name of Move	Controller Command
Side Breaker	Hold Ⓐ + Ⓐ
Steinerline	Hold Ⓐ + ⇑ + Ⓐ
Inside Side Buster	Hold Ⓐ + ⇓ + Ⓐ
Belly to Belly Suplex	Hold Ⓐ + Ⓑ
Canadian Backbreaker	Hold Ⓐ + ⇑ + Ⓑ
Power Jack	Hold Ⓐ + ⇓ + Ⓑ

Rear Grapples—Strong

Name of Move	Controller Command
Dragon Suplex	Hold Ⓐ + Ⓐ
German Suplex	Hold Ⓐ + Ⓑ

Whip to Ropes

Name of Move	Controller Command
Shoulder Drop	Hold Ⓐ + D Pad toward ropes + ▼ + Tap Ⓐ
Power Slam	Hold Ⓐ + D Pad toward ropes + ▼ + ⇑ + Tap Ⓐ
Power Lift Body Slam	Hold Ⓐ + D Pad toward ropes + ▼ + Hold Ⓐ
Spinning Backbreaker	Hold Ⓐ + D Pad toward ropes + ▼ + ⇑ + Hold Ⓐ

Special Attacks (When Spirit Meter Is Flashing)

FROM THE FRONT

Name of Move	Controller Command
Power Bomb	Hold Ⓐ + Analog Stick

FROM THE REAR

Name of Move	Controller Command
Drop German Suplex	Hold Ⓐ + Analog Stick

Opponent on Mat

FACE UP

Name of Move	Controller Command
Eye Gouge Submission	move near head, Tap Ⓐ
Boston Crab	move near legs, Tap Ⓐ
Elbow Drop	Tap Ⓑ

FACE DOWN

Name of Move	Controller Command
Camel Clutch	move near head, Tap Ⓐ
Knee Bar	move near legs, Tap Ⓐ
Falling Elbow	Tap Ⓑ

Rope and Turnbuckle Moves

OPPONENT ON MAT

Name of Move	Controller Command
Flying Elbow	move into turnbuckle + ▼

OPPONENT STANDING

Name of Move	Controller Command
Flying Tackle	move into turnbuckle + ▼
Pit Bull	run toward ropes, ⇑ + Ⓐ

THROW GROGGY OPPONENT INTO TURNBUCKLE

Name of Move	Controller Command
Pit Bull	Tap Ⓐ + Ⓐ
Avalanche Suplex	Hold Ⓐ + Ⓐ
Steiner Suplex	Hold Ⓐ + ⇑ + Ⓐ

RIC FLAIR

Height: 6' 1"

Weight: 243 lbs.

Signature Moves: Flying Knee Drop,
 Figure Four Leg Lock

Profile

Stylin' and profilin' to an unprecedented 13 world championships, "Nature Boy" Ric Flair is one of the greatest wrestlers of all time. Flair's incredible matches and charismatic interviews destine him for wrestling immortality. His breathtaking entrances, glittering robes, and blond mane, as well as his feared figure-four leg lock, flying knee drop, and cocky ring strut—all are patented "Nature Boy."

Punching and Kicking Moves

Name of Move	Controller Command
Straight Fist	Tap Ⓑ close
Kick	Tap Ⓑ far
Throat Chop	⇑ + Tap Ⓑ close
Knee Kick	⇑ + Tap Ⓑ far
Spinning Punch	Hold Ⓑ
Drop Kick	⇑ + Hold Ⓑ

Front Grapples—Weak

Name of Move	Controller Command
Flair Punch	Tap Ⓐ + Ⓐ
Forearm Smash	Tap Ⓐ + ⇑ + Ⓐ
Snap Mare	Tap Ⓐ + ⇓ + Ⓐ
Elbow Smash	Tap Ⓐ + Ⓑ
Aerial Brain Buster	Tap Ⓐ + ⇑ + Ⓑ
Pile Driver	Tap Ⓐ + ⇓ + Ⓑ

Rear Grapples—Weak

Name of Move	Controller Command
Back Drop	Tap Ⓐ + Ⓐ
Knee Breaker	Tap Ⓐ + Ⓑ

Front Grapples—Strong

Name of Move	Controller Command
Flying Major	Hold Ⓐ + Ⓐ
Revolution Takedown	Hold Ⓐ + ⇑ + Ⓐ
Brain Buster	Hold Ⓐ + ⇓ + Ⓐ
Double Arm Suplex	Hold Ⓐ + Ⓑ
Vertical Brain Buster	Hold Ⓐ + ⇑ + Ⓑ
Small Package Press	Hold Ⓐ + ⇓ + Ⓑ

Rear Grapples—Strong

Name of Move	Controller Command
Atomic Drop	Hold Ⓐ + Ⓐ
Abdominal Stretch	Hold Ⓐ + Ⓑ

Whip to Ropes

Name of Move	Controller Command
Shoulder Toss	Hold Ⓐ + D Pad toward ropes + ▼ + Tap Ⓐ
Arm-Drag Takedown	Hold Ⓐ + D Pad toward ropes + ▼ + ⇑ + Tap Ⓐ
Manhattan Drop	Hold Ⓐ + D Pad toward ropes + ▼ + Hold Ⓐ
Fireman's Carry	Hold Ⓐ + D Pad toward ropes + ▼ + ⇑ + Hold Ⓐ

Special Attacks (When Spirit Meter Is Flashing)

FROM THE FRONT

Name of Move	Controller Command
Sucker Punch	Hold Ⓐ + Analog Stick

FROM THE REAR

Name of Move	Controller Command
Command Performance	Hold Ⓐ + Analog Stick

Opponent on Mat

FACE UP

Name of Move	Controller Command
Eye Gouge Submission	move near head, Tap Ⓐ
Figure Four Leg Lock	move near legs, Tap Ⓐ
Elbow Drop	Tap Ⓑ

FACE DOWN

Name of Move	Controller Command
Camel Clutch	move near head, Tap Ⓐ
Cobra Twist	move near legs, Tap Ⓐ
Falling Elbow	Tap Ⓑ

Rope and Turnbuckle Moves

OPPONENT ON MAT

Name of Move	Controller Command
Flying Knee	move into turnbuckle + ▼
Flying Flair	move into turnbuckle + ▼

OPPONENT STANDING

Name of Move	Controller Command
Double Ax Handle	move into turnbuckle + ▼

THROW GROGGY OPPONENT INTO TURNBUCKLE

Name of Move	Controller Command
Turnbuckle Throat Chop	Tap Ⓐ + Ⓐ
Turnbuckle Shoulder Ram	Hold Ⓐ + Ⓐ
Riding Punch	Hold Ⓐ + ⇑ + Ⓐ

ULTIMO DRAGON

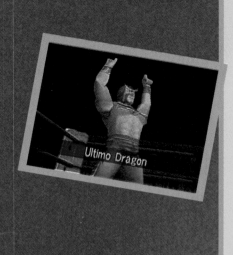

Ultimo Dragon

Height: 5' 7"

Weight: 175 lbs.

Signature Move: Dragon Sleeper

Profile

A name that is known the world over, Ultimo Dragon was born in Japan, migrated to Mexico, and is now a top wrestler in WCW! He can claim the prestigious honor of holding nine belts at the same time. This masked, adept mat technician is a well-balanced wrestler, knocking out opponents with lethal kicks and high-flying rope work.

Punching and Kicking Moves

Name of Move	Controller Command
Karate Punch	Tap Ⓑ close
Karate Kick	Tap Ⓑ far
Karate Chop	⇑ + Tap Ⓑ close
Roundhouse	⇑ + Tap Ⓑ far
Drop Kick	Hold Ⓑ
Reverse Spinning Drop Kick	⇑ + Hold Ⓑ

Front Grapples—Weak

Name of Move	Controller Command
European Upper Cut	Tap Ⓐ + Ⓐ
Snap Mare	Tap Ⓐ + ⇑ + Ⓐ
Body Drop Takedown	Tap Ⓐ + ⇓ + Ⓐ
Armwhip Elbow	Tap Ⓐ + Ⓑ
Snap Suplex	Tap Ⓐ + ⇑ + Ⓑ
Ultimodriver	Tap Ⓐ + ⇓ + Ⓑ

Rear Grapples—Weak

Name of Move	Controller Command
Reverse Back Breaker	Tap Ⓐ + Ⓐ
Savage Kick	Tap Ⓐ + Ⓑ

Front Grapples—Strong

Name of Move	Controller Command
Side Suplex	Hold Ⓐ + Ⓐ
Vertical Brain Buster	Hold Ⓐ + ⇑ + Ⓐ
Tombstone	Hold Ⓐ + ⇓ + Ⓐ
Drop DDT	Hold Ⓐ + Ⓑ
Belly to Back Suplex	Hold Ⓐ + ⇑ + Ⓑ
Grapple Doctor Bomb	Hold Ⓐ + ⇓ + Ⓑ

Rear Grapples—Strong

Name of Move	Controller Command
German Suplex	Hold Ⓐ + Ⓐ
Maya Crossarm Suplex	Hold Ⓐ + Ⓑ

Whip to Ropes

Name of Move	Controller Command
Shoulder Carry	Hold Ⓐ + D Pad toward ropes + ▼ + Tap Ⓐ
Leg Whip	Hold Ⓐ + D Pad toward ropes + ▼ + ⇑ + Tap Ⓐ
Leg Lariat	Hold Ⓐ + D Pad toward ropes + ▼ + Hold Ⓐ
Helicopter Back Breaker	Hold Ⓐ + D Pad toward ropes + ▼ + ⇑ + Hold Ⓐ

Special Attacks (When Spirit Meter Is Flashing)

FROM THE FRONT

Name of Move	Controller Command
Running Power Bomb	Hold Ⓐ + Analog Stick

FROM THE REAR

Name of Move	Controller Command
La Mahistral	Hold Ⓐ + Analog Stick

Opponent on Mat

FACE UP

Name of Move	Controller Command
Dragon Sleeper	move near head, Tap Ⓐ
Dragon Stretch	move near legs, Tap Ⓐ
Sunset Flip Drop	Tap Ⓑ

FACE DOWN

Name of Move	Controller Command
Camel Clutch	move near head, Tap Ⓐ
Surfboard Stretch	move near legs, Tap Ⓐ
Heel Stomp	Tap Ⓑ

Rope and Turnbuckle Moves

OPPONENT ON MAT

Name of Move	Controller Command
Cancun Tornado	move into turnbuckle + ▼

OPPONENT STANDING

Name of Move	Controller Command
Spinning Dragon Kick	move into turnbuckle + ▼

MOONSAULT

Name of Move	Controller Command
Asai Moonsault	run toward ropes, ⇑ + Ⓐ

THROW GROGGY OPPONENT INTO TURNBUCKLE

Name of Move	Controller Command
Karate Chop	Tap Ⓐ + Ⓐ
Suplex	Hold Ⓐ + Ⓐ
Dragonsteiner	Hold Ⓐ + ⇑ + Ⓐ

DEAN MALENKO

Height: 5' 9"
Weight: 205 lbs.
Signature Move: Texas Cloverleaf

Profile

Dean Malenko has a counter for every move, a defense for every attack, and an escape for every pinning combination. When it comes to finishing off an opponent, the end can come at any time from anywhere. This savvy ring veteran was born with wrestling in his veins. The son of the late Professor Boris Malenko, a major star in the 1960s and '70s, young Dean was schooled in the finer points of the grappling game. He is especially proficient in the art of submission and mat-based wrestling.

Punching and Kicking Moves

Name of Move	Controller Command
Elbow Smash	Tap Ⓑ close
Sharp Low Kick	Tap Ⓑ far
Hooked Slap	⇑ + Tap Ⓑ close
Middle Kick	⇑ + Tap Ⓑ far
Low Drop Kick	Hold Ⓑ
High Drop Kick	⇑ + Hold Ⓑ

Front Grapples—Weak

Name of Move	Controller Command
Forearm Smash	Tap Ⓐ + Ⓐ
Snap Mare	Tap Ⓐ + ⇑ + Ⓐ
Body Slam	Tap Ⓐ + ⇓ + Ⓐ
Reverse Arm Bar	Tap Ⓐ + Ⓑ
Brainbuster to Bodyslam	Tap Ⓐ + ⇑ + Ⓑ
Pile Driver	Tap Ⓐ + ⇓ + Ⓑ

Rear Grapples—Weak

Name of Move	Controller Command
Spinning Back Drop	Tap Ⓐ + Ⓐ
Reverse Back Breaker	Tap Ⓐ + Ⓑ

Front Grapples—Strong

Name of Move	Controller Command
Double Arm Suplex	Hold Ⓐ + Ⓐ
Fireman's Drop	Hold Ⓐ + ⇑ + Ⓐ
Power Slam	Hold Ⓐ + ⇓ + Ⓐ
Bryant Suplex	Hold Ⓐ + Ⓑ
Vertical Brain Buster	Hold Ⓐ + ⇑ + Ⓑ
Small Package Press	Hold Ⓐ + ⇓ + Ⓑ

Rear Grapples—Strong

Name of Move	Controller Command
Abdominal Stretch	Hold Ⓐ + Ⓐ
German Suplex	Hold Ⓐ + Ⓑ

Whip to Ropes

Name of Move	Controller Command
Leg Whip	Hold Ⓐ + D Pad toward ropes + ▼ + Tap Ⓐ
Body Toss	Hold Ⓐ + D Pad toward ropes + ▼ + ⇑ + Tap Ⓐ
Spinning Back Breaker	Hold Ⓐ + D Pad toward ropes + ▼ + Hold Ⓐ
Leg Lariat	Hold Ⓐ + D Pad toward ropes + ▼ + ⇑ + Hold Ⓐ

Special Attacks (When Spirit Meter Is Flashing)

FROM THE FRONT

Name of Move	Controller Command
Double Arm Power Bomb	Hold Ⓐ + Analog Stick

FROM THE REAR

Name of Move	Controller Command
Tiger Suplex	Hold Ⓐ + Analog Stick

Opponent on Mat

FACE UP

Name of Move	Controller Command
Arm Bar	move near head, Tap Ⓐ
Texas Cloverleaf	move near legs, Tap Ⓐ
Stomp	Tap Ⓑ

FACE DOWN

Name of Move	Controller Command
Camel Clutch	move near head, Tap Ⓐ
Side Surfboard Stretch	move near legs, Tap Ⓐ
Falling Elbow	Tap Ⓑ

Rope and Turnbuckle Moves

OPPONENT ON MAT

Name of Move	Controller Command
Flying Elbow	move into turnbuckle + ▼

OPPONENT STANDING

Name of Move	Controller Command
Missile Kick	move into turnbuckle + ▼

THROW GROGGY OPPONENT INTO TURNBUCKLE

Name of Move	Controller Command
Corner Maul	Tap Ⓐ + Ⓐ
Avalanche Suplex	Hold Ⓐ + Ⓐ
Falling Reverse Suplex	Hold Ⓐ + ⇑ + Ⓐ

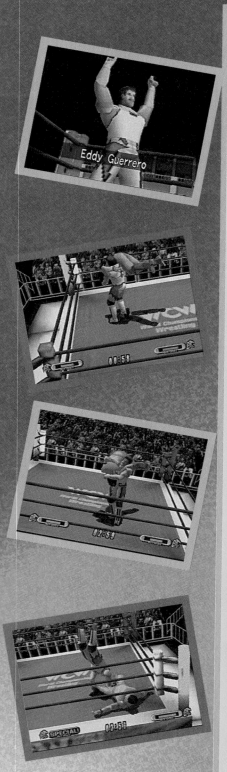

EDDY GUERRERO

Height: 5' 9"
Weight: 205 lbs.
Signature Move: Frog Splash

Profile

Hotter than a rattlesnake in the Texas sun, Eddie Guerrero, a native of El Paso, Texas, has everyone in WCW taking notice. His risky, relentless mix of aerial attacks and mat-wrestling maneuvers keeps opponents constantly off balance. He's a versatile competitor who can adapt his style to suit virtually any opponent.

Punching and Kicking Moves

Name of Move	Controller Command
Chop	Tap Ⓑ close
Mid Kick	Tap Ⓑ far
Straight Punch	⇑ + Tap Ⓑ close
Knee Kick	⇑ + Tap Ⓑ far
Super Kick	Hold Ⓑ
Drop Kick	⇑ + Hold Ⓑ

Front Grapples—Weak

Name of Move	Controller Command
Face Rake	Tap Ⓐ + Ⓐ
Snap Mare	Tap Ⓐ + ⇑ + Ⓐ
Body Slam	Tap Ⓐ + ⇓ + Ⓐ
Arm Drag Smash	Tap Ⓐ + Ⓑ
Snap Suplex	Tap Ⓐ + ⇑ + Ⓑ
Shoulder Breaker	Tap Ⓐ + ⇓ + Ⓑ

Rear Grapples—Weak

Name of Move	Controller Command
Back Drop	Tap Ⓐ + Ⓐ
Stampede	Tap Ⓐ + Ⓑ

Front Grapples—Strong

Name of Move	Controller Command
Overhead Toss	Hold Ⓐ + Ⓐ
Vertical Brain Buster	Hold Ⓐ + ⇑ + Ⓐ
Piledriver	Hold Ⓐ + ⇓ + Ⓐ
Belly to Back Suplex	Hold Ⓐ + Ⓑ
Frankensteiner	Hold Ⓐ + ⇑ + Ⓑ
Power Bomb	Hold Ⓐ + ⇓ + Ⓑ

Rear Grapples—Strong

Name of Move	Controller Command
Reverse Brainbuster	Hold Ⓐ + Ⓐ
German Suplex	Hold Ⓐ + Ⓑ

Whip to Ropes

Name of Move	Controller Command
Arm-Drag Takedown	Hold Ⓐ + D Pad toward ropes + ▼ + Tap Ⓐ
Body Toss	Hold Ⓐ + D Pad toward ropes + ▼ + ⇑ + Tap Ⓐ
Satellite Scissors	Hold Ⓐ + D Pad toward ropes + ▼ + Hold Ⓐ
Leg Lariat	Hold Ⓐ + D Pad toward ropes + ▼ + ⇑ + Hold Ⓐ

Special Attacks (When Spirit Meter Is Flashing)

FROM THE FRONT

Name of Move	Controller Command
DJ Bomb	Hold Ⓐ + Analog Stick

FROM THE REAR

Name of Move	Controller Command
Full Nelson Suplex	Hold Ⓐ + Analog Stick

Opponent on Mat

FACE UP

Name of Move	Controller Command
Knee Drop	move near head, Tap Ⓐ
Leg Crush	move near legs, Tap Ⓐ
Frog Flip	Tap Ⓑ

FACE DOWN

Name of Move	Controller Command
Camel Clutch	move near head, Tap Ⓐ
Knee Stretch	move near legs, Tap Ⓐ
Boot Stomp	Tap Ⓑ

Rope and Turnbuckle Moves

OPPONENT ON MAT

Name of Move	Controller Command
Frog Splash	(opponent square with turnbuckle) move into turnbuckle + press ▼
Diving Head Butt	move into turnbuckle + ▼

OPPONENT STANDING

Name of Move	Controller Command
Top Rope Clothesline	move into turnbuckle + ▼

MOONSAULT

Name of Move	Controller Command
Frog Somersault	run toward ropes, ⇑ + Ⓐ

THROW GROGGY OPPONENT INTO TURNBUCKLE

Name of Move	Controller Command
Riding Punch	Tap Ⓐ + Ⓐ
Top Rope Frankensteiner	Hold Ⓐ + Ⓐ
Avalanche DJ Bomb	Hold Ⓐ + ⇑ + Ⓐ

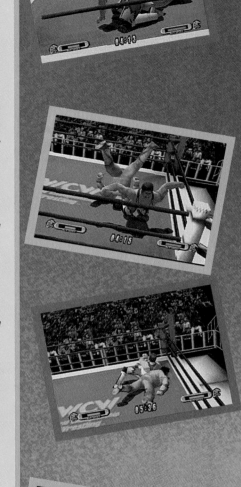

REY MYSTERIO, JR.

Height: 5' 6"

Weight: 155 lbs.

Signature Move: Hurricanrana Pin

Profile

This high-flying dynamo is unquestionably the most exciting, spell-binding wrestler in the world. His acrobatic attacks and breathtaking countermoves spring off the ring ropes as if from a taut bow. His withering, relentless attacks of high-risk maneuvers have paid off handsomely with championship success for Rey Mysterio, Jr.; he won WCW Cruiserweight belt against veteran Dean Malenko.

Punching and Kicking Moves

Name of Move	Controller Command
Forearm Punch	Tap Ⓑ close
Roundhouse	Tap Ⓑ far
Kenpo Punch	⇑ + Tap Ⓑ close
Mid Kick	⇑ + Tap Ⓑ far
Spinning Reverse Drop Kick	Hold Ⓑ
Drop Kick	⇑ + Hold Ⓑ

Front Grapples—Weak

Name of Move	Controller Command
Forearm Smash	Tap Ⓐ + Ⓐ
Snap Mare	Tap Ⓐ + ⇑ + Ⓐ
Falling Arm-Drag	Tap Ⓐ + ⇓ + Ⓐ
Elbow Grease	Tap Ⓐ + Ⓑ
Cyclone Spin	Tap Ⓐ + ⇑ + Ⓑ
Screwdriver Slam	Tap Ⓐ + ⇓ + Ⓑ

Rear Grapples—Weak

Name of Move	Controller Command
Spinning Mule Kick	Tap Ⓐ + Ⓐ
Face Crusher	Tap Ⓐ + Ⓑ

Front Grapples—Strong

Name of Move	Controller Command
Spinning Foot Lock	Hold Ⓐ + Ⓐ
Reverse Hurricanrana	Hold Ⓐ + ⇑ + Ⓐ
Head Spin Flip	Hold Ⓐ + ⇓ + Ⓐ
Suplex Press	Hold Ⓐ + Ⓑ
Hurricane Pin	Hold Ⓐ + ⇑ + Ⓑ
Small Package Press	Hold Ⓐ + ⇓ + Ⓑ

Rear Grapples—Strong

Name of Move	Controller Command
Reverse Hurricane Pin	Hold Ⓐ + Ⓐ
Cancun Flip	Hold Ⓐ + Ⓑ

Whip to Ropes

Name of Move	Controller Command
Leg Trip	Hold Ⓐ + D Pad toward ropes + ▼ + Tap Ⓐ
Overhead Toss	Hold Ⓐ + D Pad toward ropes + ▼ + ⇑ + Tap Ⓐ
Leg Lariat	Hold Ⓐ + D Pad toward ropes + ▼ + Hold Ⓐ
Spinning Back Breaker	Hold Ⓐ + D Pad toward ropes + ▼ + ⇑ + Hold Ⓐ

Special Attacks (When Spirit Meter Is Flashing)

FROM THE FRONT

Name of Move	Controller Command
Power Jack	Hold Ⓐ + Analog Stick

FROM THE REAR

Name of Move	Controller Command
Hurricanrana Pin	Hold Ⓐ + Analog Stick

Opponent on Mat

FACE UP

Name of Move	Controller Command
Side Headlock	move near head, Tap Ⓐ
Spinning Knee Crush	move near legs, Tap Ⓐ
Body Flip	Tap Ⓑ

FACE DOWN

Name of Move	Controller Command
Camel Clutch	move near head, Tap Ⓐ
Leg Lock	move near legs, Tap Ⓐ
Falling Elbow	Tap Ⓑ

Rope and Turnbuckle Moves

OPPONENT ON MAT

Name of Move	Controller Command
Sunset Pin	(opponent square with turnbuckle) move into turnbuckle + ▼
Cancun Tornado	move into turnbuckle + ▼

OPPONENT STANDING

Name of Move	Controller Command
Tope Con Hero	move into turnbuckle + ▼

MOONSAULT

Name of Move	Controller Command
Cyclone Splash	run toward ropes, ⇑ + Ⓐ

THROW GROGGY OPPONENT INTO TURNBUCKLE

Name of Move	Controller Command
Turnbuckle Tackle	Tap Ⓐ + Ⓐ
Turnbuckle Punch	Tap Ⓐ + Ⓑ
Flying Mysterio	Hold Ⓐ + Ⓐ
Flying DDT	Hold Ⓐ + ⇑ + Ⓐ

CHRIS BENOIT

Height: 5' 10"

Weight: 220 lbs.

Signature Move: Diving Headbutt

Profile

Aptly named the "Crippler," Chris Benoit fights with the eye-blinking quickness of a mongoose with many devastating weapons at his disposal. The native of Edmonton, Alberta is one of the game's most technically accomplished wrestlers. His alliance with the famed Four Horsemen alone speaks for the respect he's earned so rapidly in WCW.

Punching and Kicking Moves

Name of Move	Controller Command
Body Elbow	Tap Ⓑ close
Knee Kick	Tap Ⓑ far
Chest Slap	⇑ + Tap Ⓑ close
Karate Kick	⇑ + Tap Ⓑ far
Shoulder Charge	Hold Ⓑ
Drop Kick	⇑ + Hold Ⓑ

Front Grapples—Weak

Name of Move	Controller Command
Flying Forearm	Tap Ⓐ + Ⓐ
Head Butt	Tap Ⓐ + ⇑ + Ⓐ
Body Slam	Tap Ⓐ + ⇓ + Ⓐ
Spinal Elbow	Tap Ⓐ + Ⓑ
Snap Suplex	Tap Ⓐ + ⇑ + Ⓑ
Double Arm Power Bomb	Tap Ⓐ + ⇓ + Ⓑ

Rear Grapples—Weak

Name of Move	Controller Command
Reverse Back Breaker	Tap Ⓐ + Ⓐ
Side Suplex	Tap Ⓐ + Ⓑ

Front Grapples—Strong

Name of Move	Controller Command
Gut Wrench Suplex	Hold Ⓐ + Ⓐ
Twist Back Drop	Hold Ⓐ + ⇑ + Ⓐ
Held Tombstone	Hold Ⓐ + ⇓ + Ⓐ
Standing Clothesline	Hold Ⓐ + Ⓑ
Belly to Belly Press	Hold Ⓐ + ⇑ + Ⓑ
Power Bomb Press	Hold Ⓐ + ⇓ + Ⓑ

Rear Grapples—Strong

Name of Move	Controller Command
Reverse Brain Buster	Hold Ⓐ + Ⓐ
German Suplex	Hold Ⓐ + Ⓑ

Whip to Ropes

Name of Move	Controller Command
Arm-Drag Takedown	Hold Ⓐ + D Pad toward ropes + ▼ + Tap Ⓐ
Monkey Flip	Hold Ⓐ + D Pad toward ropes + ▼ + ⇑ + Tap Ⓐ
Body Toss	Hold Ⓐ + D Pad toward ropes + ▼ + Hold Ⓐ
Side Buster Spin	Hold Ⓐ + D Pad toward ropes + ▼ + ⇑ + Hold Ⓐ

Special Attacks (When Spirit Meter Is Flashing)

FROM THE FRONT

Name of Move	Controller Command
Power Jack	Hold Ⓐ + Analog Stick

FROM THE REAR

Name of Move	Controller Command
Full Nelson Suplex	Hold Ⓐ + Analog Stick

Opponent on Mat

FACE UP

Name of Move	Controller Command
Side Headlock	move near head, Tap Ⓐ
Boston Crab	move near legs, Tap Ⓐ
Stomp	Tap Ⓑ

FACE DOWN

Name of Move	Controller Command
Camel Clutch	move near head, Tap Ⓐ
Leg Lock	move near legs, Tap Ⓐ
Elbow Drop	Tap Ⓑ

Rope and Turnbuckle Moves

OPPONENT ON MAT

Name of Move	Controller Command
Diving Headbutt	move into turnbuckle + ▼

OPPONENT STANDING

Name of Move	Controller Command
Guillotine Drop	move into turnbuckle + ▼

THROW GROGGY OPPONENT INTO TURNBUCKLE

Name of Move	Controller Command
Corner Crunch	Tap Ⓐ + Ⓐ
Turnbuckle Pike	Tap Ⓐ + Ⓐ
Avalanche Suplex	Hold Ⓐ + Ⓐ
Dragonsteiner	Hold Ⓐ + ⇑ + Ⓐ

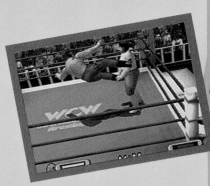

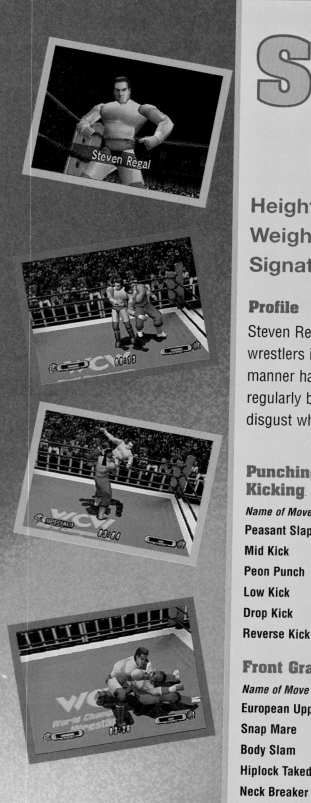

STEVEN REGAL

Height: 6' 4"

Weight: 243 lbs.

Signature Move: Regal Stretch

Profile

Steven Regal doesn't just expect to be considered one of the finest wrestlers in WCW, he believes it to be his birthright. Regal's pompous manner has not won him many allies within the ranks of WCW. He regularly belittles other wrestlers, and turns up his nose with bitter disgust when approached by fans.

Punching and Kicking Moves

Name of Move	Controller Command
Peasant Slap	Tap Ⓑ close
Mid Kick	Tap Ⓑ far
Peon Punch	⇑ + Tap Ⓑ close
Low Kick	⇑ + Tap Ⓑ far
Drop Kick	Hold Ⓑ
Reverse Kick	⇑ + Hold Ⓑ

Front Grapples—Weak

Name of Move	Controller Command
European Uppercut	Tap Ⓐ + Ⓐ
Snap Mare	Tap Ⓐ + ⇑ + Ⓐ
Body Slam	Tap Ⓐ + ⇓ + Ⓐ
Hiplock Takedown	Tap Ⓐ + Ⓑ
Neck Breaker	Tap Ⓐ + ⇑ + Ⓑ
Holding Arm Bar	Tap Ⓐ + ⇓ + Ⓑ

Rear Grapples—Weak

Name of Move	Controller Command
Back Drop	Tap Ⓐ + Ⓐ
Back Breaker	Tap Ⓐ + Ⓑ

Front Grapples—Strong

Name of Move	Controller Command
Chicken Wing Suplex	Hold Ⓐ + Ⓐ
Aerial Brain Buster	Hold Ⓐ + ⇑ + Ⓐ
Shoulder Slide Press	Hold Ⓐ + ⇓ + Ⓐ
Belly to Belly Suplex	Hold Ⓐ + Ⓑ
Arm Breaker	Hold Ⓐ + ⇑ + Ⓑ
Regal Roll	Hold Ⓐ + ⇓ + Ⓑ

Rear Grapples—Strong

Name of Move	Controller Command
Abdominal Stretch	Hold Ⓐ + Ⓐ
German Suplex	Hold Ⓐ + Ⓑ

Whip to Ropes

Name of Move	Controller Command
Overhead Drop	Hold Ⓐ + D Pad toward ropes + ▼ + Tap Ⓐ
Arm-Drag Takedown	Hold Ⓐ + D Pad toward ropes + ▼ + ⇑ + Tap Ⓐ
Cross Arm Bar	Hold Ⓐ + D Pad toward ropes + ▼ + Hold Ⓐ
Spinning Back Breaker	Hold Ⓐ + D Pad toward ropes + ▼ + ⇑ + Hold Ⓐ

Special Attacks (When Spirit Meter Is Flashing)

FROM THE FRONT

Name of Move	Controller Command
Power Bomb	Hold Ⓐ + Analog Stick

FROM THE REAR

Name of Move	Controller Command
Command Performance	Hold Ⓐ + Analog Stick

Opponent on Mat

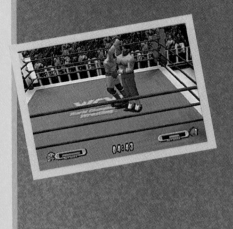

FACE UP

Name of Move	Controller Command
Reverse Head Lock	move near head, Tap Ⓐ
Regal Stretch	move near legs + Press Ⓐ
Knee Drop	Tap Ⓑ

FACE DOWN

Name of Move	Controller Command
Camel Clutch	move near head, Tap Ⓐ
Side Surfboard Stretch	move near legs, Tap Ⓐ
Royal Stomp	Tap Ⓑ

Rope and Turnbuckle Moves

OPPONENT ON MAT

Name of Move	Controller Command
Flying Elbow	move into turnbuckle + ▼

OPPONENT STANDING

Name of Move	Controller Command
Double Hammer Hand	move into turnbuckle + ▼

THROW GROGGY OPPONENT INTO TURNBUCKLE

Name of Move	Controller Command
Turnbuckle Beating	Tap Ⓐ + Ⓐ
Pub Brawl	Tap Ⓐ + Ⓑ
Avalanche Brain Buster	Hold Ⓐ + Ⓐ
Avalanche Suplex	Hold Ⓐ + ⇑ + Ⓐ

NWO

The wrestlers of NWO were once part of WCW, but they got tired of making a lot of money for other people. They decided to pursue their dream—to start a wrestling organization of their own, and vowed that one day soon they'd take over WCW wholly and utterly.

NWO (New World Order) was cofounded by pro wrestlers Kevin Nash and Scott Hall on July 7, 1996 when they, along with Hulk Hogan, took on Sting, Lex Luger, and Randy Savage in the "Bash at the Beach '96." When Hulk Hogan beat the Giant in "Hog Wild '96" that following August to win WCW World Title, Hogan used a can of spray paint to "rename" the belt "NWO World Heavyweight Title."

The wrestlers of NWO apply an "aggressive, take-charge approach" to everything they do. They train hard, work hard, and play hard, as well. Most of all, NWO wrestlers are proud to declare they're the "kind of guys who like to say 'we told you so.'"

"HOLLYWOOD" HOGAN

Height: 6' 7'

Weight: 275 lbs.

Signature Move: Top Rope Stinky Leg Drop

Profile

"Hollywood" Hulk Hogan is unquestionably the most famous contemporary wrestler in the world. He's rewriting wrestling's future as the leader of New World Order (NWO). After making the industry what it is today, Hulk is doing things his way. Dressed in NWO black, "Hollywood" Hogan, Kevin Nash, and Scott Hall have staggered WCW with their challenge for supremacy.

Punching and Kicking Moves

Name of Move	Controller Command
Uppercut	Tap Ⓑ close
Knee Kick	Tap Ⓑ far
Body Blow	⇑ + Tap Ⓑ close
Cruiser Kick	⇑ + Tap Ⓑ far
Python Punch	Hold Ⓑ
Hollywood Kick	⇑ + Hold Ⓑ

Front Grapples—Weak

Name of Move	Controller Command
Headlock Punch	Tap Ⓐ + Ⓐ
Body Slam	Tap Ⓐ + ⇑ + Ⓐ
Knee Butt	Tap Ⓐ + ⇓ + Ⓐ
Hiplock Takedown	Tap Ⓐ + Ⓑ
Armlock Smash	Tap Ⓐ + ⇑ + Ⓑ
Pile Driver	Tap Ⓐ + ⇓ + Ⓑ

Rear Grapples—Weak

Name of Move	Controller Command
Backdrop	Tap Ⓐ + Ⓐ
Atomic Knee	Tap Ⓐ + Ⓑ

Front Grapples—Strong

Name of Move	Controller Command
Top Rope Clothesline	Hold Ⓐ + Ⓐ
Vertical Brain Buster	Hold Ⓐ + ⇑ + Ⓐ
Neck Breaker	Hold Ⓐ + ⇓ + Ⓐ
Hollywood Clothesline	Hold Ⓐ + Ⓑ
Power Lift Body Slam	Hold Ⓐ + ⇑ + Ⓑ

Rear Grapples—Strong

Name of Move	Controller Command
Chicken Wing Stretch	Hold Ⓐ + Ⓐ
Hogan Back Breaker	Hold Ⓐ + Ⓑ

Whip to Ropes

Name of Move	Controller Command
Shoulder Lift	Hold Ⓐ + D Pad toward ropes + ▼ + Tap Ⓐ
Arm-Drag Takedown	Hold Ⓐ + D Pad toward ropes + ▼ + ⇑ + Tap Ⓐ
Hulk Bomber	Hold Ⓐ + D Pad toward ropes + ▼ + Hold Ⓐ
Sleeper Hold	Hold Ⓐ + D Pad toward ropes + ▼ + ⇑ + Hold Ⓐ

Special Attacks (When Spirit Meter Is Flashing)

FROM THE FRONT

Name of Move	Controller Command
Choke Hold	Hold Ⓐ + Analog Stick

FROM THE REAR

Name of Move	Controller Command
Reverse Small Package Press	Hold Ⓐ + Analog Stick

Opponent on Mat

FACE UP

Name of Move	Controller Command
Side Headlock	move near head, Tap Ⓐ
Leg Crusher	move near legs, Tap Ⓐ
Leg Drop	Tap Ⓑ

FACE DOWN

Name of Move	Controller Command
Camel Clutch	move near head, Tap Ⓐ
Boston Crab	move near legs, Tap Ⓐ
Elbow Drop	Tap Ⓑ

Rope and Turnbuckle Moves

OPPONENT ON MAT

Name of Move	Controller Command
Top Rope Stinky Leg Drop	move into turnbuckle + ▼

OPPONENT STANDING

Name of Move	Controller Command
Hulk Hammer	move into turnbuckle + ▼

THROW GROGGY OPPONENT INTO TURNBUCKLE

Name of Move	Controller Command
Riding Punch	Tap Ⓐ + Ⓐ
Avalanche Brain Buster	Hold Ⓐ + Ⓐ

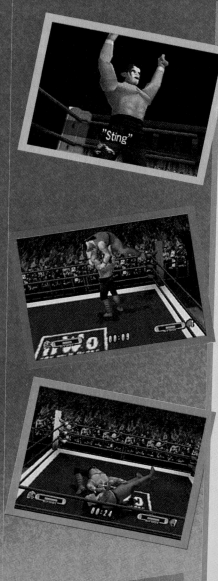

"STING"

Height: 6' 2"

Weight: 260 lbs.

Signature Move: Scorpion Death Lock

Profile

In a pathetic attempt to embarrass the WCW superstar, NWO has created its own version of Sting. This weakling has attempted to confuse fans and foes alike, but no imitation can match the power of the Stinger.

Punching and Kicking Moves

Name of Move	Controller Command
Ear Elbow	Tap Ⓑ close
Knee Kick	Tap Ⓑ far
Crown Knuckle	⇑ + Tap Ⓑ close
Soccer Kick	⇑ + Tap Ⓑ far
Drop Kick	Hold Ⓑ
Stinger Punch	⇑ + Hold Ⓑ

Front Grapples—Weak

Name of Move	Controller Command
Hammer Punch	Tap Ⓐ + Ⓐ
Shoulder Carry	Tap Ⓐ + ⇑ + Ⓐ
Body Slam	Tap Ⓐ + ⇓ + Ⓐ
Headlock Sweep	Tap Ⓐ + Ⓑ
Lifting Slam	Tap Ⓐ + ⇑ + Ⓑ
Back Buster	Tap Ⓐ + ⇓ + Ⓑ

Rear Grapples—Weak

Name of Move	Controller Command
Face Crusher	Tap Ⓐ + Ⓐ
Backdrop	Tap Ⓐ + Ⓑ

Front Grapples—Strong

Name of Move	Controller Command
Inside Side Buster	Hold Ⓐ + Ⓐ
Belly to Belly Suplex	Hold Ⓐ + ⇑ + Ⓐ
Power Bomb	Hold Ⓐ + ⇓ + Ⓐ
DDT	Hold Ⓐ + Ⓑ
Vertical Brain Buster	Hold Ⓐ + ⇑ + Ⓑ
Small Package Press	Hold Ⓐ + ⇓ + Ⓑ

Rear Grapples—Strong

Name of Move	Controller Command
Scorpion Death Drop	Hold Ⓐ + Ⓐ
Throw German Suplex	Hold Ⓐ + Ⓑ

Whip to Ropes

Name of Move	Controller Command
Arm-Drag Takedown	Hold Ⓐ + D Pad toward ropes + ▼ + Tap Ⓐ
Shoulder Slam	Hold Ⓐ + D Pad toward ropes + ▼ + ⇑ + Tap Ⓐ
Power Lift Body Slam	Hold Ⓐ + D Pad toward ropes + ▼ + Hold Ⓐ
Manhattan Drop	Hold Ⓐ + D Pad toward ropes + ▼ + ⇑ + Hold Ⓐ

Special Attacks (When Spirit Meter Is Flashing)

FROM THE FRONT

Name of Move	Controller Command
Power Jack	Hold Ⓐ + Analog Stick

FROM THE REAR

Name of Move	Controller Command
German Suplex	Hold Ⓐ + Analog Stick

Opponent on Mat

FACE UP

Name of Move	Controller Command
Side Headlock	move near head, Tap Ⓐ
Scorpion Death Lock	move near legs, Tap Ⓐ
Stomp	Tap Ⓑ

FACE DOWN

Name of Move	Controller Command
Camel Clutch	move near head, Tap Ⓐ
Leg Lock	move near legs, Tap Ⓐ
Crushing Knee	Tap Ⓑ

Rope and Turnbuckle Moves

OPPONENT ON MAT

Name of Move	Controller Command
Flying Knee	move into turnbuckle + ▼

OPPONENT STANDING

Name of Move	Controller Command
Diving Clothesline	move into turnbuckle + ▼

THROW GROGGY OPPONENT INTO TURNBUCKLE

Name of Move	Controller Command
Turnbuckle Slam	Tap Ⓐ + Ⓐ
Avalanche Suplex	Hold Ⓐ + Ⓐ
Super Brain-Buster	Hold Ⓐ + ⇑ + Ⓐ
Stinger Splash	D Pad + ▼ + Ⓑ

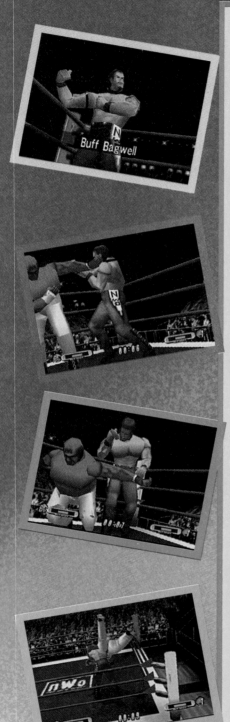

BUFF BAGWELL

Height: 6' 1"

Weight: 247 lbs.

Signature Move: Manhattan Drop

Profile

For most of his youthful career, Marcus "Buff" Bagwell was WCW's golden boy. He was named WCW Rookie of the Year and won three WCW World Tag Team titles with three different partners. Now, having seen the light and joining NWO, Bagwell has jettisoned his ripped wrecking-ball bod to another level. In a strap-match, cage, tag-team, or singles brawl, Bagwell brings serious beef to NWO.

Punching and Kicking Moves

Name of Move	Controller Command
Crown Elbow	Tap Ⓑ close
Knee Kick	Tap Ⓑ far
Chest Chop	⇑ + Tap Ⓑ close
Karate Kick	⇑ + Tap Ⓑ far
Low Drop Kick	Hold Ⓑ
Bionic Punch	⇑ + Hold Ⓑ

Front Grapples—Weak

Name of Move	Controller Command
Elbow Smash	Tap Ⓐ + Ⓐ
One-Handed Hammer Blow	Tap Ⓐ + ⇑ + Ⓐ
Body Slam	Tap Ⓐ + ⇓ + Ⓐ
Arm-Drag Elbow	Tap Ⓐ + Ⓑ
Snap Suplex	Tap Ⓐ + ⇑ + Ⓑ
Power Slam	Tap Ⓐ + ⇓ + Ⓑ

Rear Grapples—Weak

Name of Move	Controller Command
Backdrop	Tap Ⓐ + Ⓐ
Reverse Clothesline	Tap Ⓐ + Ⓑ

Front Grapples—Strong

Name of Move	Controller Command
Neck Breaker	Hold Ⓐ + Ⓐ
Standing Clothesline	Hold Ⓐ + ⇑ + Ⓐ
Tilt-a-Whirl Piledriver	Hold Ⓐ + ⇓ + Ⓐ
DDT	Hold Ⓐ + Ⓑ
Reverse Karate Kick	Hold Ⓐ + ⇑ + Ⓑ
Small Package Press	Hold Ⓐ + ⇓ + Ⓑ

Rear Grapples—Strong

Name of Move	Controller Command
Sleeper Hold	Hold Ⓐ + Ⓐ
German Suplex	Hold Ⓐ + Ⓑ

Whip to Ropes

Name of Move	Controller Command
Shoulder Drop	Hold Ⓐ + D Pad toward ropes + ▼ + Tap Ⓐ
Arm-Drag Takedown	Hold Ⓐ + D Pad toward ropes + ▼ + ⇑ + Tap Ⓐ
Power Lift Body Slam	Hold Ⓐ + D Pad toward ropes + ▼ + Hold Ⓐ
Manhattan Drop	Hold Ⓐ + D Pad toward ropes + ▼ + ⇑ + Hold Ⓐ

Special Attacks (When Spirit Meter Is Flashing)

FROM THE FRONT

Name of Move	Controller Command
Fisherman's Suplex	Hold Ⓐ + Analog Stick

FROM THE REAR

Name of Move	Controller Command
Grapple Doctor Bomb	Hold Ⓐ + Analog Stick

Opponent on Mat

FACE UP

Name of Move	Controller Command
Knee Drop	move near head, Tap Ⓐ
Target Drop	move near legs, Tap Ⓐ
Falling Elbow	Tap Ⓑ

FACE DOWN

Name of Move	Controller Command
Camel Clutch	move near head, Tap Ⓐ
Knee Wrench	near legs, Tap Ⓐ
Super Stomp	Tap Ⓑ

Rope and Turnbuckle Moves

OPPONENT ON MAT

Name of Move	Controller Command
Flying Elbow	move into turnbuckle + ▼

OPPONENT STANDING

Name of Move	Controller Command
Somersault Splash	move into turnbuckle + ▼

MOONSAULT

Name of Move	Controller Command
Flying Reverse Body Block	run toward ropes, ⇑ + Ⓐ

THROW GROGGY OPPONENT INTO TURNBUCKLE

Name of Move	Controller Command
Turnbuckle Rampage	Tap Ⓐ + Ⓐ
Super Plex	Hold Ⓐ + Ⓐ
Bionic Brain-Buster	Hold Ⓐ + ⇑ + Ⓐ

Eric Bischoff

ERIC BISCHOFF

Height: 6'
Weight: 185 lbs.
Signature Moves: Headlock Punch,
Face Rake

Profile

Eric Bischoff is one of the most powerful men in wrestling today, earning him Richter-scale levels cheers and jeers. After directing the success of WCW as executive vice-president and general manager by attracting the greatest superstars, finding the best young talent, and creating the hottest prime-time show on basic cable—*WCW Monday Nitro Live on TNT*—Bischoff jumped aboard New World Order (NWO). Joining "Hollywood" Hulk Hogan, Kevin Nash, Scott Hall, Syxx, and Ted Dibiase, Eric Bischoff spearheaded the episodic drama of NWO's hostile takeover of WCW.

Punching and Kicking Moves

Name of Move	Controller Command
Frail Fist	Tap Ⓑ close
Groin Kick	Tap Ⓑ far
Punch	⇑+ Tap Ⓑ close
Stomach Kick	⇑ + Tap Ⓑ far
High Kick	Hold Ⓑ
Wind-Up Punch	⇑ + Hold Ⓑ

Front Grapples—Weak

Name of Move	Controller Command
Facial	Tap Ⓐ + Ⓐ
Face Rake	Tap Ⓐ + ⇑ + Ⓐ
Elbow Drop	Tap Ⓐ + ⇓ + Ⓐ
Headlock Sweep	Tap Ⓐ + Ⓑ

Rear Grapple—Weak

Name of Move	Controller Command
Forearm Smash	Tap Ⓐ + Ⓐ

Front Grapples—Strong

Name of Move	Controller Command
Headlock Punch	Hold Ⓐ + Ⓐ
Small Package Press	Hold Ⓐ + Ⓑ

Rear Grapple—Strong

Name of Move	Controller Command
Back Kick	Ⓐ + Ⓐ

Whip to Ropes

Name of Move	Controller Command
Shoulder Drop	Hold Ⓐ + D Pad toward ropes + ▼ + Tap Ⓐ
Shoulder Lift	Hold Ⓐ + D Pad toward ropes + ▼ + ⇑ + Tap Ⓐ
Sleeper Hold	Hold Ⓐ + D Pad toward ropes + ▼ + Hold Ⓐ

Special Attacks (When Spirit Meter Is Flashing)

FROM THE FRONT

Name of Move	Controller Command
Spinning Takedown	Hold Ⓐ + Analog Stick

FROM THE REAR

Name of Move	Controller Command
Sneaky Sleeper	Hold Ⓐ + Analog Stick

Opponent on Mat

FACE UP

Name of Move	Controller Command
Eye Gouge Submission	move near head, Tap Ⓐ
Leg Crush	move near legs, Tap Ⓐ
Stomp	Tap Ⓑ

FACE DOWN

Name of Move	Controller Command
Camel Clutch	move near head, Tap Ⓐ
Leg Twist	move near legs, Tap Ⓐ
Elbow Drop	Tap Ⓑ

Rope and Turnbuckle Moves

OPPONENT ON MAT

Name of Move	Controller Command
Crowd Taunt	move into turnbuckle + ▼

OPPONENT STANDING

Name of Move	Controller Command
Crowd Taunt	move into turnbuckle + ▼

THROW GROGGY OPPONENT INTO TURNBUCKLE

Name of Move	Controller Command
Turnbuckle Tackle	Tap Ⓐ + Ⓐ

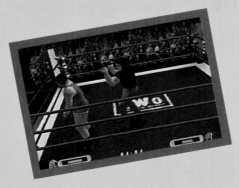

SCOTT NORTON

Height: 6' 3"

Weight: 335 lbs.

Signature Move: Shoulder Breaker

Profile

Get out of the way, the freight train is stepping into the ring. The strength of this power wrestler has his opponents shaking in their boots.

Punching and Kicking Moves

Name of Move	Controller Command
Blast Punch	Tap Ⓑ close
Kick	Tap Ⓑ far
Blast Chop	⇑ + Tap Ⓑ close
Knee Kick	⇑ + Tap Ⓑ far
Forearm Smash	Hold Ⓑ
Shoulder Charge	⇑ + Hold Ⓑ

Front Grapples—Weak

Name of Move	Controller Command
Forearm Club	Tap Ⓐ + Ⓐ
Elbow Spike	Tap Ⓐ + ⇑ + Ⓐ
Body Slam	Tap Ⓐ + ⇓ + Ⓐ
Neck Breaker	Tap Ⓐ + Ⓑ
Norton Suplex	Tap Ⓐ + ⇑ + Ⓑ
Shoulder Breaker	Tap Ⓐ + ⇓ + Ⓑ

Rear Grapples—Weak

Name of Move	Controller Command
Back Blow	Tap Ⓐ + Ⓐ
Back Drop	Tap Ⓐ + Ⓑ

Front Grapples—Strong

Name of Move	Controller Command
Standing Clothesline	Hold Ⓐ + Ⓐ
Power Lift Slam	Hold Ⓐ + ⇑ + Ⓐ
Power Slam	Hold Ⓐ + ⇓ + Ⓐ
DDT	Hold Ⓐ + Ⓑ
Choke Hold	Hold Ⓐ + ⇑ + Ⓑ
Power Bomb	Hold Ⓐ + ⇓ + Ⓑ

Rear Grapples—Strong

Name of Move	Controller Command
Throw German Suplex	Hold Ⓐ + Ⓐ
Doctor Bomb	Hold Ⓐ + Ⓑ

Whip to Ropes

Name of Move	Controller Command
Shoulder Drop	Hold Ⓐ + D Pad toward ropes + ▼ + Tap Ⓐ
Arm-drag Takedown	Hold Ⓐ + D Pad toward ropes + ▼ + ⇑ + Tap Ⓐ
Power Slam	Hold Ⓐ + D Pad toward ropes + ▼ + Hold Ⓐ
Shoulder Slam	Hold Ⓐ + D Pad toward ropes + ▼ + ⇑ + Hold Ⓐ

Special Attacks (When Spirit Meter Is Flashing)

FROM THE FRONT

Name of Move	Controller Command
Power Bomb	Hold Ⓐ + Analog Stick

FROM THE REAR

Name of Move	Controller Command
Back Drop Suplex	Hold Ⓐ + Analog Stick

Opponent on Mat

FACE UP

Name of Move	Controller Command
Dragon Sleeper	move near head, Tap Ⓐ
Boston Crab	move near legs, Tap Ⓐ
Elbow Drop	Tap Ⓑ

FACE DOWN

Name of Move	Controller Command
Camel Clutch	move near head, Tap Ⓐ
Leg Lock	move near legs, Tap Ⓐ
Knee Drop	Tap Ⓑ

Rope and Turnbuckle Moves

OPPONENT ON MAT

Name of Move	Controller Command
Flying Elbow	move into turnbuckle + ▼

OPPONENT STANDING

Name of Move	Controller Command
Shoulder Tackle	move into turnbuckle + ▼

THROW GROGGY OPPONENT INTO TURNBUCKLE

Name of Move	Controller Command
Open Hand Punch	Tap Ⓐ + Ⓐ
Suplex	Hold Ⓐ + Ⓐ
Avalanche Suplex	Hold Ⓐ + ⇑ + Ⓐ

KEVIN NASH

Height: 7' 1"
Weight: 367 lbs.
Signature Move: Jackknife Power Bomb

Profile

Seven-foot-one Kevin Nash is a towering measuring stick for wrestling's future. Partnered with NWO member Scott Hall as the champion tag team "The Outsiders," the two are bad-to-the-bone awesome. Nash has a "special" direct way of communicating—such as jackknifing WCW Executive VP Eric Bischoff through a table. The impact of such persuasion is amazing—Bischoff soon joined NWO. Action is one thing, but talk is something Nash works like a master. Equipped with a lightning wit and superior intelligence, Nash dishes out biting banter faster than McDonald's spews burgers. Finding humor in most things, except when he makes a joke of opponents, Nash is the soul of NWO.

Punching and Kicking Moves

Name of Move	Controller Command
Wimp Slap	Tap Ⓑ close
Stomach Kick	Tap Ⓑ far
Thunder Punch	⇑ + Tap Ⓑ close
Knee Kick	⇑ + Tap Ⓑ far
Thunder Kick	Hold Ⓑ
Haymaker	⇑ + Hold Ⓑ

Front Grapples—Weak

Name of Move	Controller Command
Elbow Smash	Tap Ⓐ + Ⓐ
One-Handed Hammer Blow	Tap Ⓐ + ⇑ + Ⓐ
Bruisin' Body Slam	Tap Ⓐ + ⇓ + Ⓐ
Headlock Sweep	Tap Ⓐ + Ⓑ
Suplex to Body Slam	Tap Ⓐ + ⇑ + Ⓑ
Knee Butt	Tap Ⓐ + ⇓ + Ⓑ

Rear Grapples—Weak

Name of Move	Controller Command
Spine Buster	Tap Ⓐ + Ⓐ
Knee Crush	Tap Ⓐ + Ⓑ

Front Grapples—Strong

Name of Move	Controller Command
Standing Clothesline	Hold Ⓐ + Ⓐ
Top Rope Clothesline	Hold Ⓐ + ⇑ + Ⓐ
Shoulder Breaker	Hold Ⓐ + ⇓ + Ⓐ
Side Buster	Hold Ⓐ + Ⓑ
Bryant Suplex	Hold Ⓐ + ⇑ + Ⓑ
Power Slam	Hold Ⓐ + ⇓ + Ⓑ

Rear Grapples—Strong

Name of Move	Controller Command
Back Breaker	Hold Ⓐ + Ⓐ
Sleeper Hold	Hold Ⓐ + Ⓑ

Whip to Ropes

Name of Move	Controller Command
Shoulder Drop	Hold Ⓐ + D Pad toward ropes + ▼ + Tap Ⓐ
Body Toss	Hold Ⓐ + D Pad toward ropes + ▼ + ⇑ + Tap Ⓐ
Running Power Slam	Hold Ⓐ + D Pad toward ropes + ▼ + Hold Ⓐ
Choke Slam	Hold Ⓐ + D Pad toward ropes + ▼ + ⇑ + Hold Ⓐ

Special Attacks (When Spirit Meter Is Flashing)

FROM THE FRONT

Name of Move	Controller Command
Jackknife Power Bomb	Hold Ⓐ + Analog Stick

FROM THE REAR

Name of Move	Controller Command
Trash Compactor	Hold Ⓐ + Analog Stick

Opponent on Mat

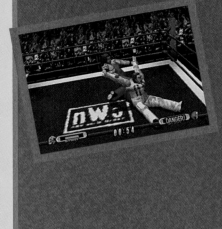

FACE UP

Name of Move	Controller Command
Surfboard	move near head, Tap Ⓐ
Knee Crusher	move near legs, Tap Ⓐ
Elbow Drop	Tap Ⓑ

FACE DOWN

Name of Move	Controller Command
Camel Clutch	move near head, Tap Ⓐ
Leg Lock	move near legs, Tap Ⓐ
Boot Stomp	Tap Ⓑ

Rope and Turnbuckle Moves

OPPONENT ON MAT

Name of Move	Controller Command
Flying Elbow	move into turnbuckle + ▼

OPPONENT STANDING

Name of Move	Controller Command
Double Axe Handle	move into turnbuckle + ▼

THROW GROGGY OPPONENT INTO TURNBUCKLE

Name of Move	Controller Command
Turnbuckle Rumble	Tap Ⓐ + Ⓐ
Bully Beat	Tap Ⓐ + Ⓑ
Top Rope Brain Buster	Hold Ⓐ + Ⓐ
Top Rope Suplex	Hold Ⓐ + ⇑ + Ⓐ

SCOTT HALL

Height: 6' 7"

Weight: 287 lbs.

Signature Pinning Move: Outsider's Edge

Profile

He's power, he's pizzazz, he's Scott Hall…the man who started it all. First he shocked the world by taking over *WCW Monday Nitro;* then he spun the planet in a *new* orbit—New World Order (NWO). No doubt, the man has stroke. With his with dark curls, five o'clock shadow, toothpick, and shades, Scott Hall even *looks* menacing, confident, and fun.

Punching and Kicking Moves

Name of Move	Controller Command
Rabbit Punch	Tap Ⓑ close
Kick	Tap Ⓑ far
Body Blow	⇑ + Tap Ⓑ close
Knee Kick	⇑ + Tap Ⓑ far
Hellion Kick	Hold Ⓑ
Crossfire Fist	⇑ + Hold Ⓑ

Front Grapples—Weak

Name of Move	Controller Command
Forearm Smash	Tap Ⓐ + Ⓐ
Eye Gouge	Tap Ⓐ + ⇑ + Ⓐ
Body Slam	Tap Ⓐ + ⇓ + Ⓐ
Elbow Smash	Tap Ⓐ + Ⓑ
Waterwheel Drop	Tap Ⓐ + ⇑ + Ⓑ
Pile Driver	Tap Ⓐ + ⇓ + Ⓑ

Rear Grapples—Weak

Name of Move	Controller Command
Spine Stunner	Tap Ⓐ + Ⓐ
Back Drop	Tap Ⓐ + Ⓑ

Front Grapples—Strong

Name of Move	Controller Command
Standing Clothesline	Hold Ⓐ + Ⓐ
Cross-Body Flip Slam	Hold Ⓐ + ⇑ + Ⓐ
Tiger Suplex	Hold Ⓐ + ⇓ + Ⓐ
Manhattan Drop	Hold Ⓐ + Ⓑ
Bryant Suplex	Hold Ⓐ + ⇑ + Ⓑ
Power Bomb	Hold Ⓐ + ⇓ + Ⓑ

Rear Grapples—Strong

Name of Move	Controller Command
Throw German Suplex	Hold Ⓐ + Ⓐ
Body Rack	Hold Ⓐ + Ⓑ

Whip to Ropes

Name of Move	Controller Command
Shoulder Drop	Hold Ⓐ + D Pad toward ropes + ▼ + Tap Ⓐ
Arm-drag Takedown	Hold Ⓐ + D Pad toward ropes + ▼ + ⇑ + Tap Ⓐ
Sleeper Hold	Hold Ⓐ + D Pad toward ropes + ▼ + Hold Ⓐ
Fireman's Carry	Hold Ⓐ + D Pad toward ropes + ▼ + ⇑ + Hold Ⓐ

Special Attacks (When Spirit Meter Is Flashing)

FROM THE FRONT

Name of Move	Controller Command
Pinning Outsider's Edge	Hold Ⓐ + Analog Stick

FROM THE REAR

Name of Move	Controller Command
Grapple Doctor Bomb	Hold Ⓐ + Analog Stick

Opponent on Mat

FACE UP

Name of Move	Controller Command
Headlock	move near head, Tap Ⓐ
Reverse Leg Lock	move near legs, Tap Ⓐ
Heel Stomp	Tap Ⓑ

FACE DOWN

Name of Move	Controller Command
Camel Clutch	move near head, Tap Ⓐ
Boston Crab	move near legs, Tap Ⓐ
Elbow Drop	Tap Ⓑ

Rope and Turnbuckle Moves

OPPONENT ON MAT

Name of Move	Controller Command
Flying Knee	move into turnbuckle + ▼

OPPONENT STANDING

Name of Move	Controller Command
Double Axe Handle	move into turnbuckle + ▼

THROW GROGGY OPPONENT INTO TURNBUCKLE

Name of Move	Controller Command
Corner Crunch	Tap Ⓐ + Ⓐ
Avalanche Suplex	Hold Ⓐ + Ⓐ
Top Rope Outsider's Edge	Hold Ⓐ + ⇑ + Ⓐ

SYXX

Height: 6' 1"
Weight: 220 lbs.
Signature Move: Standing Buzz Killer

Profile

NWO has a lucky number—Syxx. If anyone in WCW is literally gonna kick butt, it's this guy. A lethally trained black belt in tae kwon do, Syxx brings extensive martial arts training that would make Chuck Norris proud. Now his jumping spin-wheel kicks test the ability of the megatal-ented ranks of WCW Cruiserweight division.

Punching and Kicking Moves

Name of Move	Controller Command
Crown Elbow	Tap Ⓑ close
Side Kick	Tap Ⓑ far
Cruise Chop	⇑ + Tap Ⓑ close
Knee Kick	⇑ + Tap Ⓑ far
Flash Kick	Hold Ⓑ
Spinning Leg Drop	⇑ + Hold Ⓑ

Front Grapples—Weak

Name of Move	Controller Command
Forearm	Tap Ⓐ + Ⓐ
Snap Mare	Tap Ⓐ + ⇑ + Ⓐ
Body Slam	Tap Ⓐ + ⇓ + Ⓐ
Arm Lock Smash	Tap Ⓐ + Ⓑ
Snap Suplex	Tap Ⓐ + ⇑ + Ⓑ
Pile Driver	Tap Ⓐ + ⇓ + Ⓑ

Rear Grapples—Weak

Name of Move	Controller Command
Spine Stunner	Tap Ⓐ + Ⓐ
Back Drop	Tap Ⓐ + Ⓑ

Front Grapples—Strong

Name of Move	Controller Command
Overhead Slam	Hold Ⓐ + Ⓐ
Flying Guillotine	Hold Ⓐ + ⇑ + Ⓐ
Inverted Pile Driver	Hold Ⓐ + ⇓ + Ⓐ
Spinning Savate Kick	Hold Ⓐ + Ⓑ
Buzz Kill Bomb	Hold Ⓐ + ⇑ + Ⓑ
Belly to Belly Suplex	Hold Ⓐ + ⇓ + Ⓑ

Rear Grapples—Strong

Name of Move	Controller Command
Standing Buzz Killer	Hold Ⓐ + Ⓐ
German Suplex	Hold Ⓐ + Ⓑ

Whip to Ropes

Name of Move	Controller Command
Scissors Trip	Hold Ⓐ + D Pad toward ropes + ▼ + Tap Ⓐ
Arm-drag Takedown	Hold Ⓐ + D Pad toward ropes + ▼ + ⇑ + Tap Ⓐ
Body Toss	Hold Ⓐ + D Pad toward ropes + ▼ + Hold Ⓐ
Spinning Leg Lariat	Hold Ⓐ + D Pad toward ropes + ▼ + ⇑ + Hold Ⓐ

Special Attacks (When Spirit Meter Is Flashing)

FROM THE FRONT

Name of Move	Controller Command
PowerSlam Press	Hold Ⓐ + Analog Stick

FROM THE REAR

Name of Move	Controller Command
Tiger Suplex	Hold Ⓐ + Analog Stick

Opponent on Mat

FACE UP

Name of Move	Controller Command
Eye Gouge Submission	move near head, Tap Ⓐ
Leg Lock	move near legs, Tap Ⓐ
Leg Drop	Tap Ⓑ

FACE DOWN

Name of Move	Controller Command
Camel Clutch	move near head, Tap Ⓐ
Hamstring Stretch	move near legs, Tap Ⓐ
Falling Elbow	Tap Ⓑ

Rope and Turnbuckle Moves

OPPONENT ON MAT

Name of Move	Controller Command
Top Rope Leg Drop	move into turnbuckle + ▼

OPPONENT STANDING

Name of Move	Controller Command
Spinning Kick	move into turnbuckle + ▼

THROW GROGGY OPPONENT INTO TURNBUCKLE

Name of Move	Controller Command
Turnbuckle Tackle	Tap Ⓐ + Ⓐ
Dragonsteiner	Ⓐ + ⇑ + Ⓐ

DOA

Comprising former pit fighters, ultimate fighting champions, and Death Match fighters, DOA (Dead or Alive) organization proudly likens itself to the outlaws of the Old West.

SUMO JO

Height: 6' 4"
Weight: 264 lbs.
Signature Moves: Pearl Harbor,
    Kamikaze Krunch

Profile

Sporting more gross tonnage than the *Kobyashi Maru*, Sumo Jo is the most feared wrestler ever to emerge from Japan's sumo culture. A legend in his time, Sumo Jo grew tired of his life of wealth and luxury. Restless, having beaten every opponent who challenged him, Sumo Jo joined DOA to conquer a new frontier.

Punching and Kicking Moves

Name of Move	Controller Command
Sumo Slap	Tap Ⓑ close
Karate Kick	Tap Ⓑ far
Kempo Punch	⇑ + Tap Ⓑ close
Counter Kick	⇑ + Tap Ⓑ far
Drop Kick	Hold Ⓑ
Super Punch	⇑ + Hold Ⓑ

Front Grapples—Weak

Name of Move	Controller Command
Sumo Chop	Tap Ⓐ + Ⓐ
Double Chop	Tap Ⓐ + ⇑ + Ⓐ
Sumo Slam	Tap Ⓐ + ⇓ + Ⓐ
Hiplock Takedown	Tap Ⓐ + Ⓑ
Setting Sum Slam	Tap Ⓐ + ⇑ + Ⓑ
Pearl Harbor	Tap Ⓐ + ⇓ + Ⓑ

Rear Grapples—Weak

Name of Move	Controller Command
Reverse Sumo Slam	Tap Ⓐ + Ⓐ
Leg Breaker	Tap Ⓐ + Ⓑ

Front Grapples—Strong

Name of Move	Controller Command
Quadra Knee	Hold Ⓐ + Ⓐ
Triple Chop	Hold Ⓐ + ⇑ + Ⓐ
Kamikaze Krunch	Hold Ⓐ + ⇓ + Ⓐ
Kempo Face-Breaker	Hold Ⓐ + Ⓑ
Atomic Drop	Hold Ⓐ + ⇑ + Ⓑ
Atomic Bomb	Hold Ⓐ + ⇓ + Ⓑ

Rear Grapples—Strong

Name of Move	Controller Command
Club Fist	Hold Ⓐ + Ⓐ
Sumo Stretch	Hold Ⓐ + Ⓑ

Whip to Ropes

Name of Move	Controller Command
Overhead Slam	Hold Ⓐ + D Pad toward ropes + ▼ + Tap Ⓐ
Face Breaker Slam	Hold Ⓐ + D Pad toward ropes + ▼ + ⇑ + Tap Ⓐ
Japanese Sleeper	Hold Ⓐ + D Pad toward ropes + ▼ + Hold Ⓐ
Super Stretch	Hold Ⓐ + D Pad toward ropes + ▼ + ⇑ + Hold Ⓐ

Special Attacks (When Spirit Meter Is Flashing)

FROM THE FRONT

Name of Move	Controller Command
Killer Karate Kraze	Hold Ⓐ + Analog Stick

FROM THE REAR

Name of Move	Controller Command
Japanese Torture Rack	Hold Ⓐ + Analog Stick

Opponent on Mat

FACE UP

Name of Move	Controller Command
Wing-Breaker	move near head, Tap Ⓐ
Japanese Leg Breaker	move near legs, Tap Ⓐ
Floor Kick	Tap Ⓑ

FACE DOWN

Name of Move	Controller Command
Killer Clutch	move near head, Tap Ⓐ
Ankle Wrench	move near legs, Tap Ⓐ
Elbow Smash	Tap Ⓑ

Rope and Turnbuckle Moves

OPPONENT ON MAT

Name of Move	Controller Command
Flying Elbow	move into turnbuckle + ▼
Sumo Smash	move into turnbuckle + ▼

OPPONENT STANDING

Name of Move	Controller Command
Sumo Stomp	move into turnbuckle + ▼

THROW GROGGY OPPONENT INTO TURNBUCKLE

Name of Move	Controller Command
Shoulder Smash	Tap Ⓐ + Ⓐ
Karate Chop	Tap Ⓐ + Ⓑ
Flying Spinebuster	Hold Ⓐ + Ⓐ
Sump Splash	Hold Ⓐ + ⇑ + Ⓐ

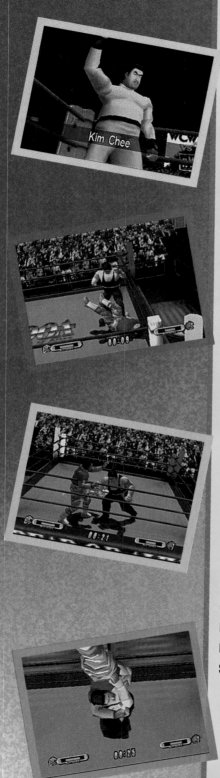

KIM CHEE

Height: 6' 9"

Weight: 194 lbs.

Signature Moves: Korean Crush,
    Turnbuckle Smash

Profile

A seasoned veteran of several hundred pit fights, Kim Chee is without a doubt Korea's most dangerous export. The mysterious, hidden arenas of Kim Chee's native land were not only his own personal "stomping" grounds, but also Kim Chee's only home: He was abandoned as a child by his parents.

Punching and Kicking Moves

Name of Move	Controller Command
Punch	Tap Ⓑ close
Mid Kick	Tap Ⓑ far
Cross Punch	⇑ + Tap Ⓑ close
Knee Kick	⇑ + Tap Ⓑ far
Korean Spike	Hold Ⓑ
Shoulder Charge	⇑ + Hold Ⓑ

Front Grapples—Weak

Name of Move	Controller Command
Backflip Throw	Tap Ⓐ + Ⓐ
Inverted Shoulder Buster	Tap Ⓐ + ⇑ + Ⓐ
Body Slam	Tap Ⓐ + ⇓ + Ⓐ
Korean Crank	Tap Ⓐ + Ⓑ
Inverse Claw Suplex	Tap Ⓐ + ⇑ + Ⓑ
Shoulder Breaker	Tap Ⓐ + ⇓ + Ⓑ

Rear Grapples—Weak

Name of Move	Controller Command
Back Spike	Tap Ⓐ + Ⓐ
Backflip Slam	Tap Ⓐ + Ⓑ

Front Grapples—Strong

Name of Move	Controller Command
Neck Breaker	Hold Ⓐ + Ⓐ
Jun Juke	Hold Ⓐ + ⇑ + Ⓐ
Power Bomb	Hold Ⓐ + ⇓ + Ⓐ
Standing Clothesline	Hold Ⓐ + Ⓑ
Turnbuckle Smash	Hold Ⓐ + ⇑ + Ⓑ
Korean Crush	Hold Ⓐ + ⇓ + Ⓑ

Rear Grapples—Strong

Name of Move	Controller Command
Chicken Wing Suplex	Hold Ⓐ + Ⓐ
Reverse Backflip Suplex	Hold Ⓐ + Ⓑ

Whip to Ropes

Name of Move	Controller Command
Shoulder Drop	Hold Ⓐ + D Pad toward ropes + ▼ + Tap Ⓐ
Press Slam	Hold Ⓐ + D Pad toward ropes + ▼ + ⇑ + Tap Ⓐ
Spine Buster	Hold Ⓐ + D Pad toward ropes + ▼ + Hold Ⓐ
Groin Buster	Hold Ⓐ + D Pad toward ropes + ▼ + ⇑ + Hold Ⓐ

Special Attacks (When Spirit Meter Is Flashing)

FROM THE FRONT

Name of Move	Controller Command
Spinning Power Slam	Hold Ⓐ + Analog Stick

FROM THE REAR

Name of Move	Controller Command
Mun Doo Mash	Hold Ⓐ + Analog Stick

Opponent on Mat

FACE UP

Name of Move	Controller Command
Headlock	move near head, Tap Ⓐ
Reverse Leg Lock	move near legs, Tap Ⓐ
Elbow Drop	Tap Ⓑ

FACE DOWN

Name of Move	Controller Command
Camel Clutch	move near head, Tap Ⓐ
Ankle Killer	move near legs, Tap Ⓐ
Super Stomp	Tap Ⓑ

Rope and Turnbuckle Moves

OPPONENT ON MAT

Name of Move	Controller Command
Flying Elbow	move into turnbuckle + ▼
Korean Splash	move into turnbuckle + ▼

OPPONENT STANDING

Name of Move	Controller Command
Flying Tackle	move into turnbuckle + ▼

THROW GROGGY OPPONENT INTO TURNBUCKLE

Name of Move	Controller Command
Dead End	Tap Ⓐ + Ⓐ
Heavy Hits	Tap Ⓐ + Ⓑ
Super Suplex	Hold Ⓐ + Ⓐ
Drop Zone	Hold Ⓐ + ⇑ + Ⓐ

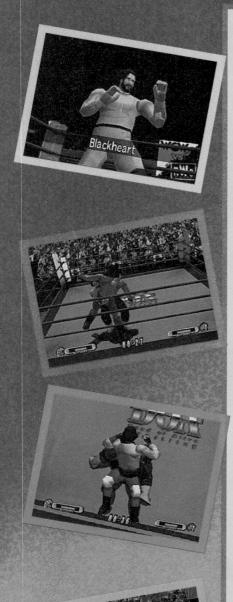

BLACKHEART

Height: 6'

Weight: 275 lbs.

Signature Move: Blackheart Back Bomb

Profile

A ferocious opponent, Blackheart rose to the top of the "underground" pit-fighting circuit the hard way—one utterly ruthless victory at a time. Blackheart's enemies know all too well the painful humiliation of a back-breaking defeat at the hands of this proud, fierce Native American pit-fighter.

Punching and Kicking Moves

Name of Move	Controller Command
Hammer Blow	Tap Ⓑ close
Kick	Tap Ⓑ far
Hatchet Blow	⇑ + Tap Ⓑ close
Mid Kick	⇑ + Tap Ⓑ far
Head Butt	Hold Ⓑ
Clothesline	⇑ + Hold Ⓑ

Front Grapples—Weak

Name of Move	Controller Command
Scalp Buster	Tap Ⓐ + Ⓐ
Forearm Club	Tap Ⓐ + ⇑ + Ⓐ
Body Slam	Tap Ⓐ + ⇓ + Ⓐ
Wrist Wrench	Tap Ⓐ + Ⓑ
ThunderBomb	Tap Ⓐ + ⇑ + Ⓑ
Pile Driver	Tap Ⓐ + ⇓ + Ⓑ

Rear Grapples—Weak

Name of Move	Controller Command
Triple Head Butt	Tap Ⓐ + Ⓐ
Spine Breaker	Tap Ⓐ + Ⓑ

Front Grapples—Strong

Name of Move	Controller Command
Headlock Crush	Hold Ⓐ + Ⓐ
Blackheart Bomb	Hold Ⓐ + ⇑ + Ⓐ
Power Bomb	Hold Ⓐ + ⇓ + Ⓐ
Neck Lynch	Hold Ⓐ + Ⓑ
Face Smash	Hold Ⓐ + ⇑ + Ⓑ
Forearm Smash	Hold Ⓐ + ⇓ + Ⓑ

Rear Grapples—Strong

Name of Move	Controller Command
Sleeper	Hold Ⓐ + Ⓐ
Shoulder Carry	Hold Ⓐ + Ⓑ

Whip to Ropes

Name of Move	Controller Command
Press Slam	Hold Ⓐ + D Pad toward ropes + ▼ + Tap Ⓐ
Power Slam	Hold Ⓐ + D Pad toward ropes + ▼ + ⇑ + Tap Ⓐ
Spine Buster	Hold Ⓐ + D Pad toward ropes + ▼ + Hold Ⓐ
Thunderbird	Hold Ⓐ + D Pad toward ropes + ▼ + ⇑ + Hold Ⓐ

Special Attacks (When Spirit Meter Is Flashing)

FROM THE FRONT

Name of Move	Controller Command
Blackheart Back Bomb	Hold Ⓐ + Analog Stick

FROM THE REAR

Name of Move	Controller Command
Face Spike	Hold Ⓐ + Analog Stick

Opponent on Mat

FACE UP

Name of Move	Controller Command
Groin Crash	move near head, Tap Ⓐ
Elbow Drop	move near legs, Tap Ⓐ
Elbow Drop	Tap Ⓑ

FACE DOWN

Name of Move	Controller Command
Desert Whip	move near head, Tap Ⓐ
Ankle Crank	move near legs, Tap Ⓐ
Falling Elbow	Tap Ⓑ

Rope and Turnbuckle Moves

OPPONENT ON MAT

Name of Move	Controller Command
Flying Elbow	move into turnbuckle + ▼
Sacrifice Splash	move into turnbuckle + ▼

OPPONENT STANDING

Name of Move	Controller Command
Double Hatchet	move into turnbuckle + ▼

THROW GROGGY OPPONENT INTO TURNBUCKLE

Name of Move	Controller Command
Turnbuckle Shoulder	Tap Ⓐ + Ⓐ
Corner Punch	Tap Ⓐ + Ⓑ
Thunder Suplex	Hold Ⓐ + Ⓐ
Flying DDT	Hold Ⓐ + ⇑ + Ⓐ

PUCHTECA

Height: 6'

Weight: 246 lbs.

Signature Moves: El Tigre Splash, Flauta Flip

Profile

Cold, cruel, and calculating, Puchteca is a true technician in every sense of the word. Infamous for never losing his cool under pressure, Puchteca's bone- and spirit-crushing techniques stem from an international blend of fighting styles, including Brazilian *capoeira* and Mexican *manos de muerte*.

Punching and Kicking Moves

Name of Move	Controller Command
Elbow	Tap Ⓑ close
Kick	Tap Ⓑ far
Straight Punch	⇑+ Tap Ⓑ close
Mid Kick	⇑ + Tap Ⓑ far
Muerte Punch	Hold Ⓑ
Drop Kick	⇑ + Hold Ⓑ

Front Grapples—Weak

Name of Move	Controller Command
Mexican Suplex	Tap Ⓐ + Ⓐ
Shoulder Throw	Tap Ⓐ + ⇑ + Ⓐ
Brazillian Head Butt	Tap Ⓐ + ⇓ + Ⓐ
Hip Toss	Tap Ⓐ + Ⓑ
Burrito Bomb	Tap Ⓐ + ⇑ + Ⓑ
Body Slam	Tap Ⓐ + ⇓ + Ⓑ

Rear Grapples—Weak

Name of Move	Controller Command
Taco Crunch	Tap Ⓐ + Ⓐ
Backflip Drop	Tap Ⓐ + Ⓑ

Front Grapples—Strong

Name of Move	Controller Command
Headlock Vise	Hold Ⓐ + Ⓐ
Flauta Flip	Hold Ⓐ + ⇑ + Ⓐ
Spine Buster	Hold Ⓐ + ⇓ + Ⓐ
Face Smash	Hold Ⓐ + Ⓑ
Avocado Crush	Hold Ⓐ + ⇑ + Ⓑ
Brazilian Bomb	Hold Ⓐ + ⇓ + Ⓑ

Rear Grapples—Strong

Name of Move	Controller Command
Abdominal Stretch	Hold Ⓐ + Ⓐ
Reverse Burrito Bomb	Hold Ⓐ + Ⓑ

Whip to Ropes

Name of Move	Controller Command
Shoulder Carry	Hold Ⓐ + D Pad toward ropes + ▼ + Tap Ⓐ
Leg Shoot	Hold Ⓐ + D Pad toward ropes + ▼ + ⇑ + Tap Ⓐ
Super Spine Buster	Hold Ⓐ + D Pad toward ropes + ▼ + Hold Ⓐ
Rio Wrench	Hold Ⓐ + D Pad toward ropes + ▼ + ⇑ + Hold Ⓐ

Special Attacks (When Spirit Meter Is Flashing)

FROM THE FRONT

Name of Move	Controller Command
Mexican Death Drop	Hold Ⓐ + Analog Stick

FROM THE REAR

Name of Move	Controller Command
Brazillian Rack	Hold Ⓐ + Analog Stick

Opponent on Mat

FACE UP

Name of Move	Controller Command
Side Headlock	move near head, Tap Ⓐ
Leg Lock	move near legs, Tap Ⓐ
Elbow Drop	Tap Ⓑ

FACE DOWN

Name of Move	Controller Command
Cancun Clutch	move near head, Tap Ⓐ
Ankle Twist	move near legs, Tap Ⓐ
Boot Stomp	Tap Ⓑ

Rope and Turnbuckle Moves

OPPONENT ON MAT

Name of Move	Controller Command
Cucaracha Crunch	move into turnbuckle + ▼
Flying Chop	move into turnbuckle + ▼

OPPONENT STANDING

Name of Move	Controller Command
NAME OF MOVE	move into turnbuckle + ▼

THROW GROGGY OPPONENT INTO TURNBUCKLE

Name of Move	Controller Command
Corner Crunch	Tap Ⓐ + Ⓐ
Street Fight Punch	Tap Ⓐ + Ⓑ
Flying DDT	Hold Ⓐ + Ⓐ
El Tigre Splash	Hold Ⓐ + ⇑ + Ⓐ

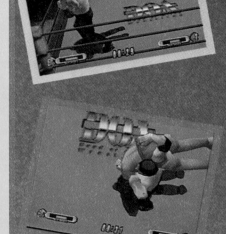

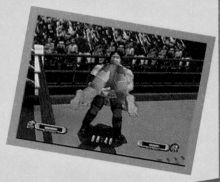

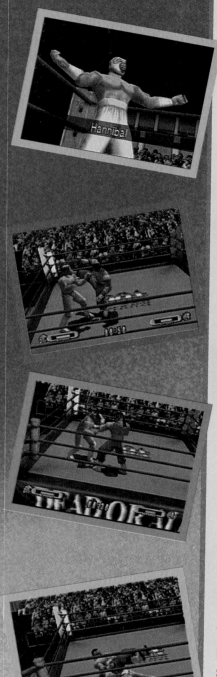

HANNIBAL

Height: 6' 1"

Weight: 233 lbs.

Signature Moves: Inverted Death Drop,
  Flying Leg Enforcer

Profile

Pulverizing his opponents with his own unique brand of fighting savagery, Hannibal is one lightweight *no one ever* takes lightly. Schooled in the unforgiving Death Match arenas of the Southwest, Hannibal never gives up, never gives in, and never admits defeat.

Punching and Kicking Moves

Name of Move	Controller Command
Claw Punch	Tap Ⓑ close
Low Kick	Tap Ⓑ far
Backhand Punch	⇑ + Tap Ⓑ close
Roundhouse Kick	⇑ + Tap Ⓑ far
Reverse Kick	Hold Ⓑ
Spin Kick	⇑ + Hold Ⓑ

Front Grapples—Weak

Name of Move	Controller Command
Throat Chop	Tap Ⓐ + Ⓐ
Lightning Throw	Tap Ⓐ + ⇑ + Ⓐ
Super Slam	Tap Ⓐ + ⇓ + Ⓐ
Headlock Toss	Tap Ⓐ + Ⓑ
Grapple Suplex	Tap Ⓐ + ⇑ + Ⓑ
Arm-Claw Hold	Tap Ⓐ + ⇓ + Ⓑ

Rear Grapples—Weak

Name of Move	Controller Command
Face Breaker	Tap Ⓐ + Ⓐ
Blackout Kick	Tap Ⓐ + Ⓑ

Front Grapples—Strong

Name of Move	Controller Command
Punisher Slam	Hold Ⓐ + Ⓐ
Super Kick	Hold Ⓐ + ⇑ + Ⓐ
Crippler Crush	Hold Ⓐ + ⇓ + Ⓐ
Knee Breaker	Hold Ⓐ + Ⓑ
Inverted Death Drop	Hold Ⓐ + ⇑ + Ⓑ
Power Slam	Hold Ⓐ + ⇓ + Ⓑ

Rear Grapples—Strong

Name of Move	Controller Command
Crusher Crunch	Hold Ⓐ + Ⓐ
Full Nelson Flip	Hold Ⓐ + Ⓑ

Whip to Ropes

Name of Move	Controller Command
Leg Whip	Hold Ⓐ + D Pad toward ropes + ▼ + Tap Ⓐ
Leg Lasso	Hold Ⓐ + D Pad toward ropes + ▼ + ⇑ + Tap Ⓐ
Back Breaker	Hold Ⓐ + D Pad toward ropes + ▼ + Hold Ⓐ
Lights Out	Hold Ⓐ + D Pad toward ropes + ▼ + ⇑ + Hold Ⓐ

Special Attacks (When Spirit Meter Is Flashing)

FROM THE FRONT

Name of Move	Controller Command
Crash Test	Hold Ⓐ + Analog Stick

FROM THE REAR

Name of Move	Controller Command
Wrist Lock	Hold Ⓐ + Analog Stick

Opponent on Mat

FACE UP

Name of Move	Controller Command
Leg Wrench	move near head, Tap Ⓐ
Booty Bomb	move near legs, Tap Ⓐ
Camel Clutch	Tap Ⓑ

FACE DOWN

Name of Move	Controller Command
Boston Crab	move near head, Tap Ⓐ
Somersault Splash	move near legs, Tap Ⓐ
Knee Drop	Tap Ⓑ

Rope and Turnbuckle Moves

OPPONENT ON MAT

Name of Move	Controller Command
Death Dive	move into turnbuckle + ▼
Spinning Kick	move into turnbuckle + ▼

OPPONENT STANDING

Name of Move	Controller Command
Rope Wrap	move into turnbuckle + ▼

MOONSAULT

Name of Move	Controller Command
Corner Charge	run toward ropes, ⇑ + Ⓐ

THROW GROGGY OPPONENT INTO TURNBUCKLE

Name of Move	Controller Command
Punching Bag	Tap Ⓐ + Ⓐ
Cranium Crash	Tap Ⓐ + Ⓑ
Flying Leg Enforcer	Hold Ⓐ + ⇑ + Ⓐ

POWDER KEG

Height: 6'

Weight: 260 lbs.

Signature Moves: Moonshine Suplex,
  Good Ol' Bomb

Profile

A rootin', tootin', good ol' boy from Drakesboro, Kentucky, Powder Keg personifies the spirit of the old Deep South moonshine runners. Taking orders from no one, answering only to himself, Powder Keg blasts the competition out of the ring every time he steps onto the apron in his size 14 boots.

Punching and Kicking Moves

Name of Move	Controller Command
Pounder	Tap Ⓑ close
Knee Kick	Tap Ⓑ far
Blast Punch	⇑+ Tap Ⓑ close
Side Kick	⇑ + Tap Ⓑ far
Head Blast	Hold Ⓑ
Clothesline	⇑ + Hold Ⓑ

Front Grapples—Weak

Name of Move	Controller Command
Head Bomb	Tap Ⓐ + Ⓐ
Powder Punch	Tap Ⓐ + ⇑ + Ⓐ
Body Slam	Tap Ⓐ + ⇓ + Ⓐ
Headlock Takedown	Tap Ⓐ + Ⓑ
Southern Suplex	Tap Ⓐ + ⇑ + Ⓑ
Pile Driver	Tap Ⓐ + ⇓ + Ⓑ

Rear Grapples—Weak

Name of Move	Controller Command
Shoulder Slam	Tap Ⓐ + Ⓐ
Triple Head Butt	Tap Ⓐ + Ⓑ

Front Grapples—Strong

Name of Move	Controller Command
Redneck Sweep	Hold Ⓐ + Ⓐ
Standing Goody	Hold Ⓐ + ⇑ + Ⓐ
Spine Buzzer	Hold Ⓐ + ⇓ + Ⓐ
Southern DDT	Hold Ⓐ + Ⓑ
Moonshine Suplex	Hold Ⓐ + ⇑ + Ⓑ
Powder Slam	Hold Ⓐ + ⇓ + Ⓑ

Rear Grapples—Strong

Name of Move	Controller Command
Abdominal Stretch	Hold Ⓐ + Ⓐ
Reverse Nitro	Hold Ⓐ + Ⓑ

Whip to Ropes

Name of Move	Controller Command
Shoulder Toss	Hold Ⓐ + D Pad toward ropes + ▼ + Tap Ⓐ
Face Bomb	Hold Ⓐ + D Pad toward ropes + ▼ + ⇑ + Tap Ⓐ
Back Smash	Hold Ⓐ + D Pad toward ropes + ▼ + Hold Ⓐ
Spine Buster	Hold Ⓐ + D Pad toward ropes + ▼ + ⇑ + Hold Ⓐ

Special Attacks (When Spirit Meter Is Flashing)

FROM THE FRONT

Name of Move	Controller Command
Good Ol' Bomb	Hold Ⓐ + Analog Stick

FROM THE REAR

Name of Move	Controller Command
Rib Rack	Hold Ⓐ + Analog Stick

Opponent on Mat

FACE UP

Name of Move	Controller Command
Face Lock	move near head, Tap Ⓐ
Low Blow	move near legs, Tap Ⓐ
Elbow Drop	Tap Ⓑ

FACE DOWN

Name of Move	Controller Command
Critter Clutch	move near head, Tap Ⓐ
Leg Vise	move near legs, Tap Ⓐ
Falling Elbow	Tap Ⓑ

Rope and Turnbuckle Moves

OPPONENT ON MAT

Name of Move	Controller Command
Flying Elbow	move into turnbuckle + ▼
Possum Drive	move into turnbuckle + ▼

OPPONENT STANDING

Name of Move	Controller Command
Super Chop	move into turnbuckle + ▼

THROW GROGGY OPPONENT INTO TURNBUCKLE

Name of Move	Controller Command
Turnbuckle Break	Tap Ⓐ + Ⓐ
Dead End Punch	Tap Ⓐ + Ⓑ
Hillbilly Heave	Hold Ⓐ + Ⓐ
Southern Super Plex	Hold Ⓐ + ⇑ + Ⓐ

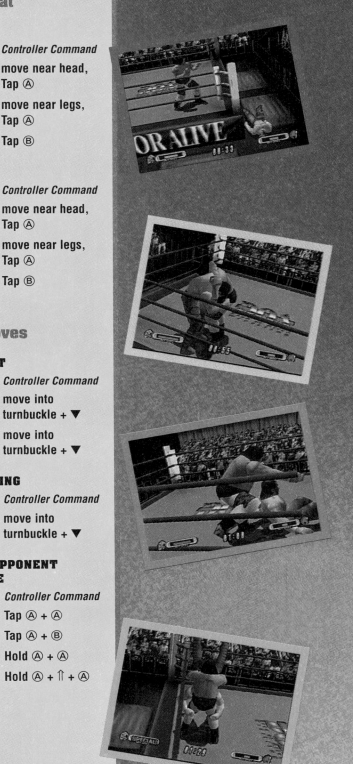

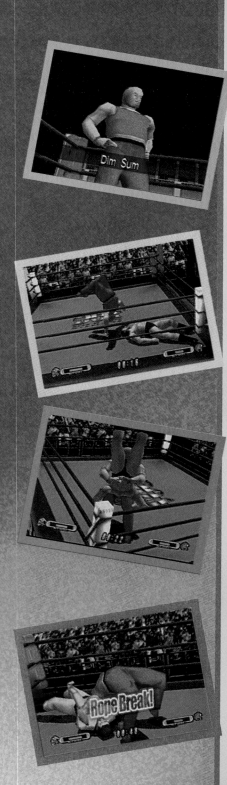

DIM SUM

Height: 5' 10"

Weight: 209 lbs.

Signature Moves: Chinese Torture Rack, Thunder Mountain

Profile

A former Olympic athlete hailed the world over for his strength and quickness, Dim Sum is China's forgotten son. A renegade government agency covertly attempted to mold him into a weapon of war, but he refused to slavishly accept their indoctrination. Dim Sum was unjustly accused of being a traitor and was ejected from his homeland.

Punching and Kicking Moves

Name of Move	Controller Command
Close Punch	Tap Ⓑ close
Mid Kick	Tap Ⓑ far
Elbow Strike	⇑ + Tap Ⓑ close
Side Kick	⇑ + Tap Ⓑ far
Mid Drop Kick	Hold Ⓑ
Reverse Backspin Kick	⇑ + Hold Ⓑ

Front Grapples—Weak

Name of Move	Controller Command
Head Butt	Tap Ⓐ + Ⓐ
China Chop	Tap Ⓐ + ⇑ + Ⓐ
Super Slam	Tap Ⓐ + ⇓ + Ⓐ
Snake Twist	Tap Ⓐ + Ⓑ
Snap Suplex	Tap Ⓐ + ⇑ + Ⓑ
Stone Driver	Tap Ⓐ + ⇓ + Ⓑ

Rear Grapples—Weak

Name of Move	Controller Command
Back Slam	Tap Ⓐ + Ⓐ
Knee Breaker	Tap Ⓐ + Ⓑ

Front Grapples—Strong

Name of Move	Controller Command
Chop Suey Slam	Hold Ⓐ + Ⓐ
Backflip	Hold Ⓐ + ⇑ + Ⓐ
Power Bomb	Hold Ⓐ + ⇓ + Ⓐ
Chinese Joint Suplex	Hold Ⓐ + Ⓑ
Giant Suplex	Hold Ⓐ + ⇑ + Ⓑ
Fortune Cookie Crunch	Hold Ⓐ + ⇓ + Ⓑ

Rear Grapples—Strong

Name of Move	Controller Command
Backflip Press	Hold Ⓐ + Ⓐ
Full Nelson Flip	Hold Ⓐ + Ⓑ

Whip to Ropes

Name of Move	Controller Command
Leg Trip	Hold Ⓐ + D Pad toward ropes + ▼ + Tap Ⓐ
Flying Crane Crank	Hold Ⓐ + D Pad toward ropes + ▼ + ⇑ + Tap Ⓐ
Thunder Mountain	Hold Ⓐ + D Pad toward ropes + ▼ + Hold Ⓐ
Bamboo Breaker Press	Hold Ⓐ + D Pad toward ropes + ▼ + ⇑ + Hold Ⓐ

Special Attacks (When Spirit Meter Is Flashing)

FROM THE FRONT

Name of Move	Controller Command
Great Wall Brain Buster	Hold Ⓐ + Analog Stick

FROM THE REAR

Name of Move	Controller Command
Chinese Leg Sweep Press	Hold Ⓐ + Analog Stick

Opponent on Mat

FACE UP

Name of Move	Controller Command
Cranium Crank	move near head, Tap Ⓐ
Pressure Point Hold	move near legs, Tap Ⓐ
Monkey Splash	Tap Ⓑ

FACE DOWN

Name of Move	Controller Command
Komodo Clutch	move near head, Tap Ⓐ
Chinese Torture Rack	move near legs, Tap Ⓐ
Monkey Flip	Tap Ⓑ

Rope and Turnbuckle Moves

OPPONENT ON MAT

Name of Move	Controller Command
Flying Head Butt	move into turnbuckle + ▼
Shoyu Splash	move into turnbuckle + ▼

OPPONENT STANDING

Name of Move	Controller Command
Kung Fu Crash	move into turnbuckle + ▼

MOONSAULT

Name of Move	Controller Command
Flying Guillotine DDT	run toward ropes, ⇑ + Ⓐ

THROW GROGGY OPPONENT INTO TURNBUCKLE

Name of Move	Controller Command
Corner Smash	Tap Ⓐ + Ⓐ
Turnbuckle Bash	Tap Ⓐ + Ⓑ
Flying Dragon DDT	Hold Ⓐ + Ⓐ
Moonsault Butt Buster	Hold Ⓐ + ⇑ + Ⓐ

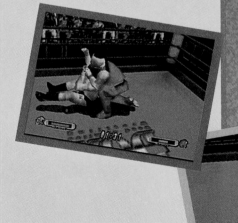

SALADIN

Height: 6' 3"

Weight: 264 lbs.

Signature Moves: Death Drop, Deadly Claw

Profile

A lone figure, standing silent as a stone sentinel on the apron, Saladin suddenly tosses his opponent clear out of the ring and onto the concrete floor. Once Afghanistan's top Secret Service operative, Saladin refused his handler's repeated attempts to induce him to assassinate Mikhail Gorbachev. Now, Saladin uses his skills to defeat, but never permanently disable, his opponents.

Punching and Kicking Moves

Name of Move	Controller Command
Shadow Punch	Tap Ⓑ close
Knife Kick	Tap Ⓑ far
Silent Strike	⇑ + Tap Ⓑ close
Reverse Jacknife	⇑ + Tap Ⓑ far
Badland Blow	Hold Ⓑ
Super Smash	⇑ + Hold Ⓑ

Front Grapples—Weak

Name of Move	Controller Command
KO Punch	Tap Ⓐ + Ⓐ
Cranium Crash	Tap Ⓐ + ⇑ + Ⓐ
Body Slam	Tap Ⓐ + ⇓ + Ⓐ
Headlock Slam	Tap Ⓐ + Ⓑ
Dark Suplex	Tap Ⓐ + ⇑ + Ⓑ
Midnight Toss	Tap Ⓐ + ⇓ + Ⓑ

Rear Grapples—Weak

Name of Move	Controller Command
Spine Strike	Tap Ⓐ + Ⓐ
Knee Drop	Tap Ⓐ + Ⓑ

Front Grapples—Strong

Name of Move	Controller Command
Neck Breaker	Hold Ⓐ + Ⓐ
Death Drop	Hold Ⓐ + ⇑ + Ⓐ
Shoulder Breaker	Hold Ⓐ + ⇓ + Ⓐ
Standing Strangle	Hold Ⓐ + Ⓑ
Super Head Butt	Hold Ⓐ + ⇑ + Ⓑ
Face Breaker	Hold Ⓐ + ⇓ + Ⓑ

Rear Grapples—Strong

Name of Move	Controller Command
Triple Head Bash	Hold Ⓐ + Ⓐ
Spinning Back Crippler	Hold Ⓐ + Ⓑ

Whip to Ropes

Name of Move	Controller Command
Shoulder Toss	Hold Ⓐ + D Pad toward ropes + ▼ + Tap Ⓐ
Body Bag Press	Hold Ⓐ + D Pad toward ropes + ▼ + ⇑ + Tap Ⓐ
Back Drop	Hold Ⓐ + D Pad toward ropes + ▼ + Hold Ⓐ
Deadly Claw	Hold Ⓐ + D Pad toward ropes + ▼ + ⇑ + Hold Ⓐ

Special Attacks (When Spirit Meter Is Flashing)

FROM THE FRONT

Name of Move	Controller Command
Choke Slam	Hold Ⓐ + Analog Stick

FROM THE REAR

Name of Move	Controller Command
Butcher Knife	Hold Ⓐ + Analog Stick

Opponent on Mat

FACE UP

Name of Move	Controller Command
Choke Hold	move near head, Tap Ⓐ
Groin Crush	move near legs, Tap Ⓐ
Falling Elbow	Tap Ⓑ

FACE DOWN

Name of Move	Controller Command
Camel Clutch	move near head, Tap Ⓐ
Leg Lock	move near legs, Tap Ⓐ
Elbow Drop	Tap Ⓑ

Rope and Turnbuckle Moves

OPPONENT ON MAT

Name of Move	Controller Command
Flying Elbow	move into turnbuckle + ▼
Saladin Splash	move into turnbuckle + ▼

OPPONENT STANDING

Name of Move	Controller Command
Flying Assassin	move into turnbuckle + ▼

THROW GROGGY OPPONENT INTO TURNBUCKLE

Name of Move	Controller Command
Corner Maul	Tap Ⓐ + Ⓐ
Turnbuckle Rampage	Tap Ⓐ + Ⓑ
Flying Death Drop	Hold Ⓐ + Ⓐ
Hangman's DDT	Hold Ⓐ + ⇑ + Ⓐ

ALI BABA

Height: 6' 4"

Weight: 264 lbs.

Signature Moves: Camel Clutch, Oasis DDT

Profile

Once a prisoner on a secret island penal colony, Ali Baba earned food rations and blankets by competing in barbarous inmate Death Matches staged by the inhuman prison warden. He escaped on the eve of his 21st birthday, swimming 17-1/2 miles to shore—and freedom. Ali Baba still proudly claims his native Turkey as his home.

Punching and Kicking Moves

Name of Move	Controller Command
Elbow	Tap Ⓑ close
Stomach Kick	Tap Ⓑ far
Punch Chop	⇑ + Tap Ⓑ close
Low Kick	⇑ + Tap Ⓑ far
Sweep Punch	Hold Ⓑ
Drop Kick	⇑ + Hold Ⓑ

Front Grapples—Weak

Name of Move	Controller Command
Eye Gouge	Tap Ⓐ + Ⓐ
Waterwheel Throw	Tap Ⓐ + ⇑ + Ⓐ
Super Slam	Tap Ⓐ + ⇓ + Ⓐ
Reverse Neck Sweep	Tap Ⓐ + Ⓑ
Sultan Suplex	Tap Ⓐ + ⇑ + Ⓑ
Brain Buster	Tap Ⓐ + ⇓ + Ⓑ

Rear Grapples—Weak

Name of Move	Controller Command
Reverse Suplex	Tap Ⓐ + Ⓐ
Knee Breaker	Tap Ⓐ + Ⓑ

Front Grapples—Strong

Name of Move	Controller Command
Chicken Wing Flip	Hold Ⓐ + Ⓐ
Lariat Takedown	Hold Ⓐ + ⇑ + Ⓐ
Hangman's Noose	Hold Ⓐ + ⇓ + Ⓐ
Skull Breaker	Hold Ⓐ + Ⓑ
Standing Choke Hold	Hold Ⓐ + ⇑ + Ⓑ
Shoulder Slide	Hold Ⓐ + ⇓ + Ⓑ

Rear Grapples—Strong

Name of Move	Controller Command
Atomic Knee	Hold Ⓐ + Ⓐ
Abdominal Rack	Hold Ⓐ + Ⓑ

Whip to Ropes

Name of Move	Controller Command
Shoulder Drop	Hold Ⓐ + D Pad toward ropes + ▼ + Tap Ⓐ
Arm-Drag Takedown	Hold Ⓐ + D Pad toward ropes + ▼ + ⇑ + Tap Ⓐ
Cranium Crusher	Hold Ⓐ + D Pad toward ropes + ▼ + Hold Ⓐ
Sheik Special	Hold Ⓐ + D Pad toward ropes + ▼ + ⇑ + Hold Ⓐ

Special Attacks (When Spirit Meter Is Flashing)

FROM THE FRONT

Name of Move	Controller Command
Choke Slam	Hold Ⓐ + Analog Stick

FROM THE REAR

Name of Move	Controller Command
Barbarian Bomb	Hold Ⓐ + Analog Stick

Opponent on Mat

FACE UP

Name of Move	Controller Command
Strangle Hold	move near head, Tap Ⓐ
Knee-Cap Smash	move near legs, Tap Ⓐ
Elbow Drop	Tap Ⓑ

FACE DOWN

Name of Move	Controller Command
Camel Clutch	move near head, Tap Ⓐ
Leg Wrench	move near legs, Tap Ⓐ
Falling Elbow	Tap Ⓑ

Rope and Turnbuckle Moves

OPPONENT ON MAT

Name of Move	Controller Command
Flying Punch	move into turnbuckle + ▼
Sultan Splash	move into turnbuckle + ▼

OPPONENT STANDING

Name of Move	Controller Command
Double Crusher	move into turnbuckle + ▼

THROW GROGGY OPPONENT INTO TURNBUCKLE

Name of Move	Controller Command
Corner Kill	Tap Ⓐ + Ⓐ
Turnbuckle Tromp	Tap Ⓐ + Ⓑ
Oasis DDT	Hold Ⓐ + Ⓐ
Avalanche Suplex	Hold Ⓐ + ⇑ + Ⓐ

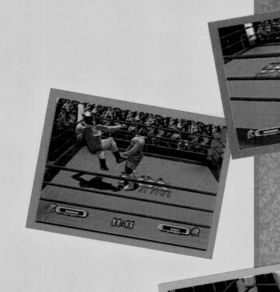

Independent Union

Absolute renegades, responsible to no one, the wrestlers of Independent Union organization do anything they want, any time they want!

BLACK NINJA

Height: 6'
Weight: 190 lbs.
Signature Moves: Flying Dragon Kick, Jaw Breaker, Wall-Walking Trample

Profile

Shrouded in mystery, cloaked in controversy, only one rumor about this legendary Independent Union Japanese fighter has been verified by Black Ninja himself. On the one occasion he's known ever to have spoken aloud, Black Ninja confirmed that he was trained *since birth* in the customs and practices of the Ninja warrior.

Punching and Kicking Moves

Name of Move	Controller Command
Karate Punch	Tap Ⓑ close
Reverse Kick	Tap Ⓑ far
Karate Strike	⇑ + Tap Ⓑ close
Side Kick	⇑ + Tap Ⓑ far
Spinning Reverse Kick	Hold Ⓑ
Flying Dragon Kick	⇑ + Hold Ⓑ

Front Grapples—Weak

Name of Move	Controller Command
Iron Fist	Tap Ⓐ + Ⓐ
Shoulder Throw	Tap Ⓐ + ⇑ + Ⓐ
Body Slam	Tap Ⓐ + ⇓ + Ⓐ
Headlock Toss	Tap Ⓐ + Ⓑ
Ninja Throw	Tap Ⓐ + ⇑ + Ⓑ
Joint Lock Takedown	Tap Ⓐ + ⇓ + Ⓑ

Rear Grapples—Weak

Name of Move	Controller Command
Jaw Breaker	Tap Ⓐ + Ⓐ
Back Drop	Tap Ⓐ + Ⓑ

Front Grapples—Strong

Name of Move	Controller Command
Flying Scissors Takedown	Hold Ⓐ + Ⓐ
Wall-Walking Trample	Hold Ⓐ + ⇑ + Ⓐ
Cyclone Pile Driver	Hold Ⓐ + ⇓ + Ⓐ
Ninja DDT	Hold Ⓐ + Ⓑ
Leg Vise Press	Hold Ⓐ + ⇑ + Ⓑ
Suplex Press	Hold Ⓐ + ⇓ + Ⓑ

Rear Grapples—Strong

Name of Move	Controller Command
Japanese Rack	Hold Ⓐ + Ⓐ
Backdrop Press	Hold Ⓐ + Ⓑ

Whip to Ropes

Name of Move	Controller Command
Leg Whip	Hold Ⓐ + D Pad toward ropes + ▼ + Tap Ⓐ
Ninja Neck Crank	Hold Ⓐ + D Pad toward ropes + ▼ + ⇑ + Tap Ⓐ
Back Breaker	Hold Ⓐ + D Pad toward ropes + ▼ + Hold Ⓐ
Leg Lariat	Hold Ⓐ + D Pad toward ropes + ▼ + ⇑ + Hold Ⓐ

Special Attacks (When Spirit Meter Is Flashing)

FROM THE FRONT

Name of Move	Controller Command
Back Breaker Bomb	Hold Ⓐ + Analog Stick

FROM THE REAR

Name of Move	Controller Command
Spirit Press	Hold Ⓐ + Analog Stick

Opponent on Mat

FACE UP

Name of Move	Controller Command
Blackout Punch	move near head, Tap Ⓐ
Spinning Leg Bar	move near legs, Tap Ⓐ
Body Drop	Tap Ⓑ

FACE DOWN

Name of Move	Controller Command
Ninja Clutch	move near head, Tap Ⓐ
Japanese Leg Lock Clutch	move near legs, Tap Ⓐ
Somersault Splash	Tap Ⓑ

Rope and Turnbuckle Moves

OPPONENT ON MAT

Name of Move	Controller Command
Iga Splash	move into turnbuckle + ▼
Suicide Somersault	move into turnbuckle + ▼

OPPONENT STANDING

Name of Move	Controller Command
Hanzo Flip	move into turnbuckle + ▼

MOONSAULT

Name of Move	Controller Command
Skywalk	run toward ropes, ⇑ + Ⓐ

THROW GROGGY OPPONENT INTO TURNBUCKLE

Name of Move	Controller Command
Turnbuckle Bruiser	Tap Ⓐ + Ⓐ
Corner Clash	Tap Ⓐ + Ⓑ
Flying Shuriken	Hold Ⓐ + Ⓐ
Deadly Rain	Hold Ⓐ + ⇑ + Ⓐ

SHAOLIN

Height: 6'
Weight: 238 lbs.
Signature Moves: Shaolin Kick,
  Master Lee's Backflip Press

Profile

Eleven years ago, Shaolin broke his vows of the warrior monk, departing the isolated Tibetan mountain fortress he called home. Shaolin swore never to return to his fatherland across the Pacific, cursing his fellow monks for being too pacifistic to be worthy holy warriors. Now the pitiless Shaolin controls every aspect of his bouts with a master's hand, showing mercy to none.

Punching and Kicking Moves

Name of Move	Controller Command
Crane Fist	Tap Ⓑ close
Crane Kick	Tap Ⓑ far
Tiger Punch	⇑ + Tap Ⓑ close
Tiger Kick	⇑ + Tap Ⓑ far
Snake Fist	Hold Ⓑ
Shaolin Kick	⇑ + Hold Ⓑ

Front Grapples—Weak

Name of Move	Controller Command
Shaolin Palm	Tap Ⓐ + Ⓐ
Shoulder Throw	Tap Ⓐ + ⇑ + Ⓐ
Body Slam	Tap Ⓐ + ⇓ + Ⓐ
Mantis Grapple Throw	Tap Ⓐ + Ⓑ
Mantis Throw	Tap Ⓐ + ⇑ + Ⓑ
Thunder Mountain	Tap Ⓐ + ⇓ + Ⓑ

Rear Grapples—Weak

Name of Move	Controller Command
Back Breaker	Tap Ⓐ + Ⓐ
Monkey Flop	Tap Ⓐ + Ⓑ

Front Grapples—Strong

Name of Move	Controller Command
Drunken Sweep	Hold Ⓐ + Ⓐ
Giant Swing Throw	Hold Ⓐ + ⇑ + Ⓐ
Stone Breaker	Hold Ⓐ + ⇓ + Ⓐ
Shaolin DDT	Hold Ⓐ + Ⓑ
Strangle Slam	Hold Ⓐ + ⇑ + Ⓑ
Heaven's Gate	Hold Ⓐ + ⇓ + Ⓑ

Rear Grapples—Strong

Name of Move	Controller Command
Willow Stretch	Hold Ⓐ + Ⓐ
Drunken Press	Hold Ⓐ + Ⓑ

Whip to Ropes

Name of Move	Controller Command
Carry the Mountain	Hold Ⓐ + D Pad toward ropes + ▼ + Tap Ⓐ
Shoulder Toss	Hold Ⓐ + D Pad toward ropes + ▼ + ⇑ + Tap Ⓐ
Running Mantis Grip	Hold Ⓐ + D Pad toward ropes + ▼ + Hold Ⓐ
Shaolin Submission Hold	Hold Ⓐ + D Pad toward ropes + ▼ + ⇑ + Hold Ⓐ

Special Attacks (When Spirit Meter Is Flashing)

FROM THE FRONT

Name of Move	Controller Command
Master Young's Power Bomb Press	Hold Ⓐ + Analog Stick

FROM THE REAR

Name of Move	Controller Command
Master Lee's Backflip Press	Hold Ⓐ + Analog Stick

Opponent on Mat

FACE UP

Name of Move	Controller Command
Chicken Wing Hold	move near head, Tap Ⓐ
Leg Smash	move near legs, Tap Ⓐ
Elbow Drop	Tap Ⓑ

FACE DOWN

Name of Move	Controller Command
Camel Clutch	move near head, Tap Ⓐ
Reverse Leg Lock	move near legs, Tap Ⓐ
Iron Head Butt	Tap Ⓑ

Rope and Turnbuckle Moves

OPPONENT ON MAT

Name of Move	Controller Command
Flying Head Butt	move into turnbuckle + ▼
Shaolin Splash	move into turnbuckle + ▼

OPPONENT STANDING

Name of Move	Controller Command
Flying Shoulder Block	move into turnbuckle + ▼

MOONSAULT

Name of Move	Controller Command
Wind Walk	run toward ropes, ⇑ + Ⓐ

THROW GROGGY OPPONENT INTO TURNBUCKLE

Name of Move	Controller Command
Turnbuckle Charge	Tap Ⓐ + Ⓐ
Turnbuckle Fist	Tap Ⓐ + Ⓑ
Holy DDT	Hold Ⓐ + Ⓐ
Final Solution	Hold Ⓐ + ⇑ + Ⓐ

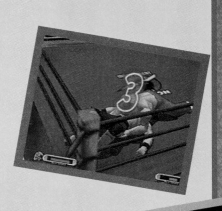

THE UNKNOWN

Height: 5' 9"

Weight: 194 lbs.

Signature Moves: Airplane Spin Back Breaker, Rampage Rocker

Profile

To pay for his father's transgressions, the Unknown spent his youth in indentured servitude—as a pit-fighter! Normally calm, quiet, and composed, he's capable of a sudden, near-homicidal rage. Truly independent in every way that matters, the Unknown is an Independent Union fighter to reckon with.

Punching and Kicking Moves

Name of Move	Controller Command
Throat Chop	Tap Ⓑ close
Kick	Tap Ⓑ far
Eye Punch	⇑ + Tap Ⓑ close
Stomach Kick	⇑ + Tap Ⓑ far
High Kick	Hold Ⓑ
Drop Kick	⇑ + Hold Ⓑ

Front Grapples—Weak

Name of Move	Controller Command
Suplex	Tap Ⓐ + Ⓐ
Snap Mare	Tap Ⓐ + ⇑ + Ⓐ
Takedown Flip	Tap Ⓐ + ⇓ + Ⓐ
Pit Bull Takedown	Tap Ⓐ + Ⓑ
Snapper Suplex	Tap Ⓐ + ⇑ + Ⓑ
Crazy Crunch	Tap Ⓐ + ⇓ + Ⓑ

Rear Grapples—Weak

Name of Move	Controller Command
Back Breaker	Tap Ⓐ + Ⓐ
Shoulder Slam	Tap Ⓐ + Ⓑ

Front Grapples—Strong

Name of Move	Controller Command
Neck Breaker	Hold Ⓐ + Ⓐ
Spinning Savate Kick	Hold Ⓐ + ⇑ + Ⓐ
Inverted Spine Buster	Hold Ⓐ + ⇓ + Ⓐ
Demented Drop	Hold Ⓐ + Ⓑ
Barbarian Break	Hold Ⓐ + ⇑ + Ⓑ
Rampage Rocker	Hold Ⓐ + ⇓ + Ⓑ

Rear Grapples—Strong

Name of Move	Controller Command
Pain Rack	Hold Ⓐ + Ⓐ
Garbage Toss	Hold Ⓐ + Ⓑ

Whip to Ropes

Name of Move	Controller Command
Arm-Drag Takedown	Hold Ⓐ + D Pad toward ropes + ▼ + Tap Ⓐ
Vicious Leg Reaper	Hold Ⓐ + D Pad toward ropes + ▼ + ⇑ + Tap Ⓐ
Airplane Spin Back Breaker	Hold Ⓐ + D Pad toward ropes + ▼ + Hold Ⓐ
Spine Buster	Hold Ⓐ + D Pad toward ropes + ▼ + ⇑ + Hold Ⓐ

Special Attacks (When Spirit Meter Is Flashing)

FROM THE FRONT

Name of Move	Controller Command
Behemoth Bomb	Hold Ⓐ + Analog Stick

FROM THE REAR

Name of Move	Controller Command
Lunatic Fling	Hold Ⓐ + Analog Stick

Opponent on Mat

FACE UP

Name of Move	Controller Command
Crazy Pretzel	move near head, Tap Ⓐ
Groin Smash	move near legs, Tap Ⓐ
Elbow Drop	Tap Ⓑ

FACE DOWN

Name of Move	Controller Command
Camel Clutch	move near head, Tap Ⓐ
Knot Lock	move near legs, Tap Ⓐ
Stomp	Tap Ⓑ

Rope and Turnbuckle Moves

OPPONENT ON MAT

Name of Move	Controller Command
Flying Elbow	move into turnbuckle + ▼
Suicide Splash	move into turnbuckle + ▼

OPPONENT STANDING

Name of Move	Controller Command
Flying Drop Kick	move into turnbuckle + ▼

MOONSAULT

Name of Move	Controller Command
Flipped Lid	run toward ropes, ⇑ + Ⓐ

THROW GROGGY OPPONENT INTO TURNBUCKLE

Name of Move	Controller Command
Turnbuckle Smash	Tap Ⓐ + Ⓐ
Corner Brawl	Tap Ⓐ + Ⓑ
Suicide DDT	Hold Ⓐ + Ⓐ
Avalanche Power Slide	Hold Ⓐ + ⇑ + Ⓐ

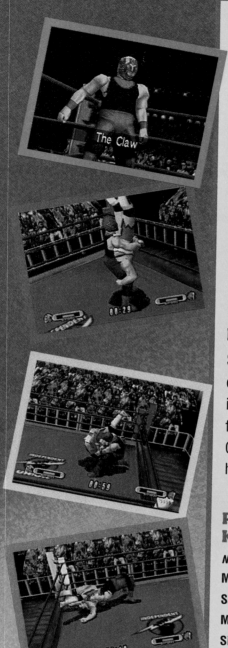

The Claw

THE CLAW

Height: 5' 11"
Weight: 213 lbs.
Signature Moves: Crossfly Crasher,
  Muerte Grip

Profile

Some people whisper that the Claw—who rose to infamy by *destroying* every challenger in the illegal Death Matches of the Georgian Republic—is actually hundreds of years old! Although this seemingly ageless fighter currently lives in an undisclosed location in New Mexico, the Claw is rumored to claim the frozen wastelands of 1064 AD Siberia as his birthplace!

Punching and Kicking Moves

Name of Move	Controller Command
Mystic Punch	Tap Ⓑ close
Savate Kick	Tap Ⓑ far
Mystic Chop	⇑ + Tap Ⓑ close
Side Kick	⇑ + Tap Ⓑ far
Flying Kick	Hold Ⓑ
Super Punch	⇑ + Hold Ⓑ

Front Grapples—Weak

Name of Move	Controller Command
Iron Claw	Tap Ⓐ + Ⓐ
Siberian Snap	Tap Ⓐ + ⇑ + Ⓐ
Ice Break Slam	Tap Ⓐ + ⇓ + Ⓐ
Bear Lock Throw	Tap Ⓐ + Ⓑ
Siberian Suplex	Tap Ⓐ + ⇑ + Ⓑ
Power Spike	Tap Ⓐ + ⇓ + Ⓑ

Rear Grapples—Weak

Name of Move	Controller Command
Lariat	Tap Ⓐ + Ⓐ
Atomic Knee	Tap Ⓐ + Ⓑ

Front Grapples—Strong

Name of Move	Controller Command
Back Breaker	Hold Ⓐ + Ⓐ
Muerte Grip	Hold Ⓐ + ⇑ + Ⓐ
Claw Twist	Hold Ⓐ + ⇓ + Ⓐ
Siberian DDT	Hold Ⓐ + Ⓑ
Leg Flip Press	Hold Ⓐ + ⇑ + Ⓑ
Power Bomb	Hold Ⓐ + ⇓ + Ⓑ

Rear Grapples—Strong

Name of Move	Controller Command
Backthrow Press	Hold Ⓐ + Ⓐ
Chicken Wing Press	Hold Ⓐ + Ⓑ

Whip to Ropes

Name of Move	Controller Command
Chain Drag	Hold Ⓐ + D Pad toward ropes + ▼ + Tap Ⓐ
Shoulder Carry	Hold Ⓐ + D Pad toward ropes + ▼ + ⇑ + Tap Ⓐ
Tundra Spin	Hold Ⓐ + D Pad toward ropes + ▼ + Hold Ⓐ
Leg Claw Throw	Hold Ⓐ + D Pad toward ropes + ▼ + ⇑ + Hold Ⓐ

Special Attacks (When Spirit Meter Is Flashing)

FROM THE FRONT

Name of Move	Controller Command
Aeon Slam	Hold Ⓐ + Analog Stick

FROM THE REAR

Name of Move	Controller Command
Crossfly Crasher	Hold Ⓐ + Analog Stick

Opponent on Mat

FACE UP

Name of Move	Controller Command
Arm Bar Hold	move near head, Tap Ⓐ
Leg Breaker	move near legs, Tap Ⓐ
Knee Smash	Tap Ⓑ

FACE DOWN

Name of Move	Controller Command
Siberian Camel Clutch	move near head, Tap Ⓐ
Tundra Twist Lock	move near legs, Tap Ⓐ
Elbow Drop	Tap Ⓑ

Rope and Turnbuckle Moves

OPPONENT ON MAT

Name of Move	Controller Command
Flying Elbow	move into turnbuckle + ▼
Siberian Splash	move into turnbuckle + ▼

OPPONENT STANDING

Name of Move	Controller Command
Flying Drop Kick	move into turnbuckle + ▼

THROW GROGGY OPPONENT INTO TURNBUCKLE

Name of Move	Controller Command
Turnbuckle Maul	Tap Ⓐ + Ⓐ
Corner Crunch	Tap Ⓐ + Ⓑ
Bear Hug Suplex	Hold Ⓐ + Ⓐ
Avalanche Splash	Hold Ⓐ + ⇑ + Ⓐ

BLACK BELT

Height: 6'

Weight: 194 lbs.

Signature Moves: Florida Flip, Commando Crunch

Profile

Notorious for his hard-hearted, relentless fighting style while wrestling for Independent Union, Black Belt has developed a reputation as a bloodthirsty opponent. A former decorated Green Beret dishonorably discharged for his murderous appetites, Black Belt lives *in* the swamps of the Florida panhandle.

Punching and Kicking Moves

Name of Move	Controller Command
Kenpo Punch	Tap Ⓑ close
Karate Kick	Tap Ⓑ far
Karate Elbow	⇑ + Tap Ⓑ close
Kenpo Kick	⇑ + Tap Ⓑ far
Dragon Kick	Hold Ⓑ
Flying Dragon Kick	⇑ + Hold Ⓑ

Front Grapples—Weak

Name of Move	Controller Command
Chi Slam	Tap Ⓐ + Ⓐ
Shoulder Throw	Tap Ⓐ + ⇑ + Ⓐ
Judo Grapple	Tap Ⓐ + ⇓ + Ⓐ
Aikido Smash	Tap Ⓐ + Ⓑ
Judo Plex	Tap Ⓐ + ⇑ + Ⓑ
Pile Driver	Tap Ⓐ + ⇓ + Ⓑ

Rear Grapples—Weak

Name of Move	Controller Command
Judo Backflip	Tap Ⓐ + Ⓐ
Karate Krash	Tap Ⓐ + Ⓑ

Front Grapples—Strong

Name of Move	Controller Command
Gut Wrench Suplex	Hold Ⓐ + Ⓐ
Spinning Kick	Hold Ⓐ + ⇑ + Ⓐ
Spinning Pile Driver	Hold Ⓐ + ⇓ + Ⓐ
Gator DDT	Hold Ⓐ + Ⓑ
Leg Flip Press	Hold Ⓐ + ⇑ + Ⓑ
Green Beret Bomb	Hold Ⓐ + ⇓ + Ⓑ

Rear Grapples—Strong

Name of Move	Controller Command
Everglade Press	Hold Ⓐ + Ⓐ
Florida Flip	Hold Ⓐ + Ⓑ

Whip to Ropes

Name of Move	Controller Command
Leg Sweep	Hold Ⓐ + D Pad toward ropes + ▼ + Tap Ⓐ
Arm-Drag Takedown	Hold Ⓐ + D Pad toward ropes + ▼ + ⇑ + Tap Ⓐ
Swamp Strangle	Hold Ⓐ + D Pad toward ropes + ▼ + Hold Ⓐ
Leg Flip Takedown	Hold Ⓐ + D Pad toward ropes + ▼ + ⇑ + Hold Ⓐ

Special Attacks (When Spirit Meter Is Flashing)

FROM THE FRONT

Name of Move	Controller Command
Commando Crunch	Hold Ⓐ + Analog Stick

FROM THE REAR

Name of Move	Controller Command
Mad Bomber	Hold Ⓐ + Analog Stick

Opponent on Mat

FACE UP

Name of Move	Controller Command
Face Punch	move near head, Tap Ⓐ
Aikido Leg Lock	move near legs, Tap Ⓐ
Elbow Drop	Tap Ⓑ

FACE DOWN

Name of Move	Controller Command
Aikido Clutch	move near head, Tap Ⓐ
Aikido Leg Twist	move near legs, Tap Ⓐ
Knee Smash	Tap Ⓑ

Rope and Turnbuckle Moves

OPPONENT ON MAT

Name of Move	Controller Command
Flying Knee	move into turnbuckle + ▼
Hitman Hurl	move into turnbuckle + ▼

OPPONENT STANDING

Name of Move	Controller Command
Jungle Jump	move into turnbuckle + ▼

MOONSAULT

Name of Move	Controller Command
Sniper Shot	run toward ropes, ⇑ + Ⓐ

THROW GROGGY OPPONENT INTO TURNBUCKLE

Name of Move	Controller Command
Trapping Charge	Tap Ⓐ + Ⓐ
Trapping Punch	Tap Ⓐ + Ⓑ
Flying Beret Bomb	Hold Ⓐ + Ⓐ
Badlands Bone Breaker	Hold Ⓐ + ⇑ + Ⓐ

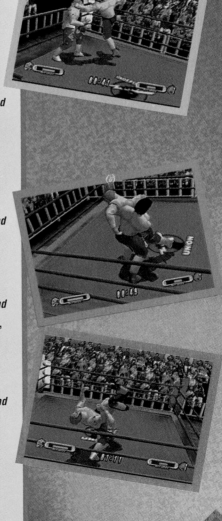

PACOLOCO

Height: 5' 9"
Weight: 220 lbs.
Signature Moves: Barrio Bomb,
California Clutch

Profile

A house favorite, PacoLoco always delivers the goods when it's go time. Trained in the school of hard knocks, PacoLoco essentially raised himself in the barrios and mean streets of Los Angeles. PacoLoco's in-your-face fighting style mixes hard-core wrestling, extreme street-fighting, and classic Greco-Roman techniques.

Punching and Kicking Moves

Name of Move	Controller Command
Jab	Tap Ⓑ close
Kick	Tap Ⓑ far
Hook Punch	⇑ + Tap Ⓑ close
Mid Kick	⇑ + Tap Ⓑ far
Roundhouse	Hold Ⓑ
Super Kick	⇑ + Hold Ⓑ

Front Grapples—Weak

Name of Move	Controller Command
Face Rip	Tap Ⓐ + Ⓐ
Shoulder Throw	Tap Ⓐ + ⇑ + Ⓐ
Body Slam	Tap Ⓐ + ⇓ + Ⓐ
Chicken Wing Throw	Tap Ⓐ + Ⓑ
Snap Suplex	Tap Ⓐ + ⇑ + Ⓑ
Barrio Buster	Tap Ⓐ + ⇓ + Ⓑ

Rear Grapples—Weak

Name of Move	Controller Command
Backstreet Slam	Tap Ⓐ + Ⓐ
Knee Busta	Tap Ⓐ + Ⓑ

Front Grapples—Strong

Name of Move	Controller Command
Clothesline Chop	Hold Ⓐ + Ⓐ
Giant Suplex	Hold Ⓐ + ⇑ + Ⓐ
Inverse Pile Driver	Hold Ⓐ + ⇓ + Ⓐ
DDT	Hold Ⓐ + Ⓑ
Hood Head Butt	Hold Ⓐ + ⇑ + Ⓑ
Funky Slam	Hold Ⓐ + ⇓ + Ⓑ

Rear Grapples—Strong

Name of Move	Controller Command
Downtown Brown	Hold Ⓐ + Ⓐ
Reverse Neck Breaker	Hold Ⓐ + Ⓑ

Whip to Ropes

Name of Move	Controller Command
Arm-Drag Takedown	Hold Ⓐ + D Pad toward ropes + ▼ + Tap Ⓐ
Paco Plunge	Hold Ⓐ + D Pad toward ropes + ▼ + ⇑ + Tap Ⓐ
Loco Moco	Hold Ⓐ + D Pad toward ropes + ▼ + Hold Ⓐ
Spine Buster	Hold Ⓐ + D Pad toward ropes + ▼ + ⇑ + Hold Ⓐ

Special Attacks (When Spirit Meter Is Flashing)

FROM THE FRONT

Name of Move	Controller Command
Houseparty Hangover	Hold Ⓐ + Analog Stick

FROM THE REAR

Name of Move	Controller Command
Barrio Bomb	Hold Ⓐ + Analog Stick

Opponent on Mat

FACE UP

Name of Move	Controller Command
Knee to the Head	move near head, Tap Ⓐ
Groin Butt	move near legs, Tap Ⓐ
Sunset Splash	Tap Ⓑ

FACE DOWN

Name of Move	Controller Command
California Clutch	move near head, Tap Ⓐ
Leg Wrench	move near legs, Tap Ⓐ
Elbow Drop	Tap Ⓑ

Rope and Turnbuckle Moves

OPPONENT ON MAT

Name of Move	Controller Command
Flying Head Butt	move into turnbuckle + ▼
Sunset Flip	move into turnbuckle + ▼

OPPONENT STANDING

Name of Move	Controller Command
Hoodlum Hit	move into turnbuckle + ▼

THROW GROGGY OPPONENT INTO TURNBUCKLE

Name of Move	Controller Command
Street Fight	Tap Ⓐ + Ⓐ
Corner Rumble	Tap Ⓐ + Ⓑ
Paco Pounce	Hold Ⓐ + Ⓐ
El Loco Suplex	Hold Ⓐ + ⇑ + Ⓐ

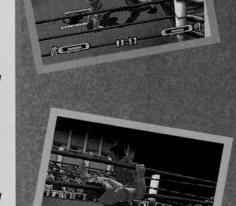

SHAMAN

Height: 6' 8"
Weight: 286 lbs.
Signature Moves: Double Tomahawk, Shaman Spike

Profile

Having followed the Way of the Warrior since he was a small boy, Shaman is a formidable opponent—unbelievably agile, ferociously strong, and incredibly tough. Although Shaman isn't above breaking a few rules (and bones) when necessary, this Native American fighter is respected by all his fellow pro wrestlers for his generosity to defeated foes.

Punching and Kicking Moves

Name of Move	Controller Command
Cross Punch	Tap Ⓑ close
Kick	Tap Ⓑ far
Tomahawk Chop	⇑ + Tap Ⓑ close
Knee Kick	⇑ + Tap Ⓑ far
Super Kick	Hold Ⓑ
Battering Ram	⇑ + Hold Ⓑ

Front Grapples—Weak

Name of Move	Controller Command
Double Tomahawk	Tap Ⓐ + Ⓐ
Stone Breaker	Tap Ⓐ + ⇑ + Ⓐ
Bear Slam	Tap Ⓐ + ⇓ + Ⓐ
Eagle Sweep	Tap Ⓐ + Ⓑ
Suplex Slam	Tap Ⓐ + ⇑ + Ⓑ
Inverted Shaman Spike	Tap Ⓐ + ⇓ + Ⓑ

Rear Grapples—Weak

Name of Move	Controller Command
Stone Forearm	Tap Ⓐ + Ⓐ
Back Drop	Tap Ⓐ + Ⓑ

Front Grapples—Strong

Name of Move	Controller Command
Eagle Drop	Hold Ⓐ + Ⓐ
Shaman Spike	Hold Ⓐ + ⇑ + Ⓐ
DDT	Hold Ⓐ + ⇓ + Ⓐ
Choke Slam	Hold Ⓐ + Ⓑ
Side Breaker Slam	Hold Ⓐ + ⇑ + Ⓑ
Power Bomb	Hold Ⓐ + ⇓ + Ⓑ

Rear Grapples—Strong

Name of Move	Controller Command
Backflip Throw	Hold Ⓐ + Ⓐ
Sideflip Throw	Hold Ⓐ + Ⓑ

Whip to Ropes

Name of Move	Controller Command
Overhead Throw	Hold Ⓐ + D Pad toward ropes + ▼ + Tap Ⓐ
Guillotine Drop	Hold Ⓐ + D Pad toward ropes + ▼ + ⇑ + Tap Ⓐ
Power Slam	Hold Ⓐ + D Pad toward ropes + ▼ + Hold Ⓐ
Spine Buster	Hold Ⓐ + D Pad toward ropes + ▼ + ⇑ + Hold Ⓐ

Special Attacks (When Spirit Meter Is Flashing)

FROM THE FRONT

Name of Move	Controller Command
Spirit Slam	Hold Ⓐ + Analog Stick

FROM THE REAR

Name of Move	Controller Command
Warpath Wrap-up	Hold Ⓐ + Analog Stick

Opponent on Mat

FACE UP

Name of Move	Controller Command
Side Headlock	move near head, Tap Ⓐ
Scorpion Death Lock	move near legs, Tap Ⓐ
Elbow Drop	Tap Ⓑ

FACE DOWN

Name of Move	Controller Command
Camel Clutch	move near head, Tap Ⓐ
Indian Knee Lock	move near legs, Tap Ⓐ
Falling Elbow	Tap Ⓑ

Rope and Turnbuckle Moves

OPPONENT ON MAT

Name of Move	Controller Command
Flying Knee	move into turnbuckle + ▼
Spirit Splash	move into turnbuckle + ▼

OPPONENT STANDING

Name of Move	Controller Command
Shaman Knee	move into turnbuckle + ▼

THROW GROGGY OPPONENT INTO TURNBUCKLE

Name of Move	Controller Command
Bear Cave	Tap Ⓐ + Ⓐ
War Cry	Tap Ⓐ + Ⓑ
Sacrifice Fly	Hold Ⓐ + Ⓐ
Shaman Suplex	Hold Ⓐ + ⇑ + Ⓐ

MASTER FUJI

Height: 6' 3"
Weight: 227 lbs.
Signature Move: Mountain Splitter

Profile

If a single wrestler can represent everything the Independent Union is all about, it's Master Fuji. Caring little for material wealth, caring less for himself, and caring not at all for other people, Master Fuji's only true love is wrestling. This Japanese fighter has forgotten more about wrestling than most other wrestlers will ever know.

Punching and Kicking Moves

Name of Move	Controller Command
Eye Punch	Tap Ⓑ close
Groin Kick	Tap Ⓑ far
Nose Punch	⇑ + Tap Ⓑ close
Knee Kick	⇑ + Tap Ⓑ far
Shoulder Charge	Hold Ⓑ
High Hit	⇑ + Hold Ⓑ

Front Grapples—Weak

Name of Move	Controller Command
Fuji Punch	Tap Ⓐ + Ⓐ
Snap Mare	Tap Ⓐ + ⇑ + Ⓐ
Fireman's Carry	Tap Ⓐ + ⇓ + Ⓐ
Side Throw	Tap Ⓐ + Ⓑ
Gut-Wrench Suplex	Tap Ⓐ + ⇑ + Ⓑ
Master Fuji's Pile Driver	Tap Ⓐ + ⇓ + Ⓑ

Rear Grapples—Weak

Name of Move	Controller Command
Triple Head Butt	Tap Ⓐ + Ⓐ
Back Breaker	Tap Ⓐ + Ⓑ

Front Grapples—Strong

Name of Move	Controller Command
Headlock Punch	Hold Ⓐ + Ⓐ
Fuji Slam	Hold Ⓐ + ⇑ + Ⓐ
Arm Bar Press	Hold Ⓐ + ⇓ + Ⓐ
Inverse Fuji Driver	Hold Ⓐ + Ⓑ
Mountain Splitter	Hold Ⓐ + ⇑ + Ⓑ
Fuji Joint Lock	Hold Ⓐ + ⇓ + Ⓑ

Rear Grapples—Strong

Name of Move	Controller Command
Neck Breaker	Hold Ⓐ + Ⓐ
Reverse Joint Lock	Hold Ⓐ + Ⓑ

Whip to Ropes

Name of Move	Controller Command
Leg Trip	Hold Ⓐ + D Pad toward ropes + ▼ + Tap Ⓐ
Fuji Flip	Hold Ⓐ + D Pad toward ropes + ▼ + ⇑ + Tap Ⓐ
Greedy Grab	Hold Ⓐ + D Pad toward ropes + ▼ + Hold Ⓐ
Japanese Sleeper Hold	Hold Ⓐ + D Pad toward ropes + ▼ + ⇑ + Hold Ⓐ

Special Attacks (When Spirit Meter Is Flashing)

FROM THE FRONT

Name of Move	Controller Command
Frontal Face Strangle	Hold Ⓐ + Analog Stick

FROM THE REAR

Name of Move	Controller Command
Fuji Bomb	Hold Ⓐ + Analog Stick

Opponent on Mat

FACE UP

Name of Move	Controller Command
Choke	move near head, Tap Ⓐ
Leg Lock	move near legs, Tap Ⓐ
Knee Drop	Tap Ⓑ

FACE DOWN

Name of Move	Controller Command
Camel Clutch	move near head, Tap Ⓐ
Joint Lock	move near legs, Tap Ⓐ
Stomp	Tap Ⓑ

Rope and Turnbuckle Moves

OPPONENT ON MAT

Name of Move	Controller Command
Flying Knee	move into turnbuckle + ▼
Fuji Splash	move into turnbuckle + ▼

OPPONENT STANDING

Name of Move	Controller Command
Flying Chop	move into turnbuckle + ▼

THROW GROGGY OPPONENT INTO TURNBUCKLE

Name of Move	Controller Command
Corner Crush	Tap Ⓐ + Ⓐ
Fuji Pummel	Tap Ⓐ + Ⓑ
Fuji Suplex	Hold Ⓐ + Ⓐ
Mt. Fuji Splash	Hold Ⓐ + ⇑ + Ⓐ

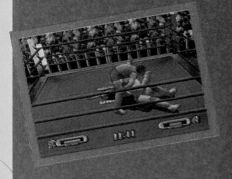

Appendix

The Bosses

Make sure your controller and Memory Pak are plugged in. Set your game for League Challenge. Defeat every wrestler in an organization to unlock the boss for that organization. Defeat all four bosses to unlock the fifth hidden organization. Beat every wrestler in World Heavyweight to get Joe Bruiser. Defeat every wrestler in World Cruiserweight to get Black Widow.

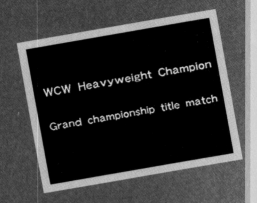

WCW Heavyweight Champion

Grand championship title match

Sting   Diamond Dallas Page

DIAMOND DALLAS PAGE (DDP)

Height: 6' 5"
Weight: 253 lbs.
Signature Move: Diamond Cutter

Profile

In recent WCW history, no one has risen to the top of the "Big Boys" faster than Diamond Dallas Page (DDP). Against the odds this color commentator-turned-manger-turned-wrestler has been a sponge for wrestling knowledge, rapidly improving with each match. His seemingly unstoppable "diamond cutter" finishing move has sliced opponents like glass. Impressive victories winning WCW TV Title and the Lord of the Ring competition have made both NWO and WCW opponents beware.

Punching and Kicking Moves

Name of Move	Controller Command
Throat Chop	Tap Ⓑ close
Mid Kick	Tap Ⓑ far
Punch	⇑ + Tap Ⓑ close
Knee Kick	⇑ + Tap Ⓑ far
Forearm Clothesline	Hold Ⓑ
Drop Kick	⇑ + Hold Ⓑ

Front Grapples—Weak

Name of Move	Controller Command
Blockbuster	Tap Ⓐ + Ⓐ
Head Butt	Tap Ⓐ + ⇑ + Ⓐ
Body Slam	Tap Ⓐ + ⇓ + Ⓐ
Diamond Elbow	Tap Ⓐ + Ⓑ
Snap Suplex	Tap Ⓐ + ⇑ + Ⓑ
Knee Butt Combo	Tap Ⓐ + ⇓ + Ⓑ

Rear Grapples—Weak

Name of Move	Controller Command
Face Crusher	Tap Ⓐ + Ⓐ
Back Drop	Tap Ⓐ + Ⓑ

Front Grapples—Strong

Name of Move	Controller Command
Inside Side Buster	Hold Ⓐ + Ⓐ
Vertical Brain Buster	Hold Ⓐ + ⇑ + Ⓐ
Piledriver to Body Slam	Hold Ⓐ + ⇓ + Ⓐ
DDT	Hold Ⓐ + Ⓑ
Backflip Slam	Hold Ⓐ + ⇑ + Ⓑ
Spinning Power Bomb	Hold Ⓐ + ⇓ + Ⓑ

Rear Grapples—Strong

Name of Move	Controller Command
Reverse Side Buster	Hold Ⓐ + Ⓐ
Grapple Doctor Bomb	Hold Ⓐ + Ⓑ

Whip to Ropes

Name of Move	Controller Command
Shoulder Throw	Hold Ⓐ + D Pad toward ropes + ▼ + Tap Ⓐ
Arm-Drag Takedown	Hold Ⓐ + D Pad toward ropes + ▼ + ⇑ + Tap Ⓐ
Power Slam	Hold Ⓐ + D Pad toward ropes + ▼ + Hold Ⓐ
Manhattan Drop	Hold Ⓐ + D Pad toward ropes + ▼ + ⇑ + Hold Ⓐ

Special Attacks (When Spirit Meter Is Flashing)

FROM THE FRONT

Name of Move	Controller Command
Diamond Cutter	Hold Ⓐ + Analog Stick

FROM THE REAR

Name of Move	Controller Command
German Suplex	Hold Ⓐ + Analog Stick

Opponent on Mat

FACE UP

Name of Move	Controller Command
Side Headlock	move near head, Tap Ⓐ
Knee Crush	move near legs, Tap Ⓐ
Elbow Drop	Tap Ⓑ

FACE DOWN

Name of Move	Controller Command
Camel Clutch	move near head, Tap Ⓐ
Leg Bar	move near legs, Tap Ⓐ
Stomp	Tap Ⓑ

Rope and Turnbuckle Moves

OPPONENT ON MAT

Name of Move	Controller Command
Flying Elbow	move into turnbuckle + ▼

OPPONENT STANDING

Name of Move	Controller Command
Diamond Dive	move into turnbuckle + ▼

THROW GROGGY OPPONENT INTO TURNBUCKLE

Name of Move	Controller Command
Turnbuckle Smash	Tap Ⓐ + Ⓐ
Corner Blitz	Tap Ⓐ + Ⓑ
Flying Brain Buster	Hold Ⓐ + Ⓐ
Avalanche DDT	Hold Ⓐ + ⇑ + Ⓐ

Diamond Dallas Page

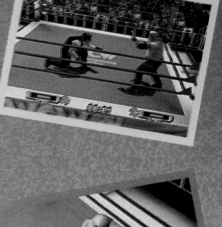

Hulk Hogan   Randy Savage

"MACHO MAN" RANDY SAVAGE

Height: 6' 1"
Weight: 230 lbs.
Signature Moves: Macho Man Flying Elbow

Profile

Wearing the wildest ring attire in wrestling and gifted with a voice that bellows like a rock 'n' roll saxophone, "Macho Man" Randy Savage is one of the most famous wrestlers in the world. The four-time world champion joined WCW seeking the best competition and accomplished his goal of winning the world title. Macho Madness now reigns in New World Order with long-time friend "Hollywood" Hulk Hogan. Before embarking on his colorful career in professional wrestling, Savage was an accomplished athlete on the baseball diamond. His transition from baseball spikes to wrestling boots has smoked with the success of a Tom Glavine fastball.

Punching and Kicking Moves

Name of Move	Controller Command
Punch	Tap Ⓑ close
Side Kick	Tap Ⓑ far
Super Chop	⇑ + Tap Ⓑ close
Knee Kick	⇑ + Tap Ⓑ far
Rolling Punch	Hold Ⓑ
Drop Kick	⇑ + Hold Ⓑ

Front Grapples—Weak

Name of Move	Controller Command
Headlock Punch	Tap Ⓐ + Ⓐ
Freaky Forearm	Tap Ⓐ + ⇑ + Ⓐ
Snap Mare	Tap Ⓐ + ⇓ + Ⓐ
Funky Elbow	Tap Ⓐ + Ⓑ
Suplex	Tap Ⓐ + ⇑ + Ⓑ
Pile Driver	Tap Ⓐ + ⇓ + Ⓑ

Rear Grapples—Weak

Name of Move	Controller Command
Back Drop	Tap Ⓐ + Ⓐ
Knee Breaker	Tap Ⓐ + Ⓑ

Front Grapples—Strong

Name of Move	Controller Command
Double Arm Suplex	Hold Ⓐ + Ⓐ
Cross Arm Combo	Hold Ⓐ + ⇑ + Ⓐ
Screwdriver Drop	Hold Ⓐ + ⇓ + Ⓐ
DDT	Hold Ⓐ + Ⓑ
Machoplex	Hold Ⓐ + ⇑ + Ⓑ
Small Package Press	Hold Ⓐ + ⇓ + Ⓑ

Rear Grapples—Strong

Name of Move	Controller Command
Atomic Drop	Hold Ⓐ + Ⓐ
Abdominal Stretch	Hold Ⓐ + Ⓑ

Whip to Ropes

Name of Move	Controller Command
Shoulder Toss	Hold Ⓐ + D Pad toward ropes + ▼ + Tap Ⓐ
Arm-Drag Takedown	Hold Ⓐ + D Pad toward ropes + ▼ + ⇑ + Tap Ⓐ
Manhattan Drop	Hold Ⓐ + D Pad toward ropes + ▼ + Hold Ⓐ
Power Slam	Hold Ⓐ + D Pad toward ropes + ▼ + ⇑ + Hold Ⓐ

Special Attacks (When Spirit Meter Is Flashing)

FROM THE FRONT

Name of Move	Controller Command
Power Bomb	Hold Ⓐ + Analog Stick

FROM THE REAR

Name of Move	Controller Command
Command Performance	Hold Ⓐ + Analog Stick

Opponent on Mat

FACE UP

Name of Move	Controller Command
Face Lock	move near head, Tap Ⓐ
Back Leg Wrench	move near legs, Tap Ⓐ
Elbow Drop	Tap Ⓑ

FACE DOWN

Name of Move	Controller Command
Camel Clutch	move near head, Tap Ⓐ
Leg Twist	move near legs, Tap Ⓐ
Falling Elbow	Tap Ⓑ

Rope and Turnbuckle Moves

OPPONENT ON MAT

Name of Move	Controller Command
Macho Man Flying Elbow	move into turnbuckle + ▼
Macho Splash	move into turnbuckle + ▼

OPPONENT STANDING

Name of Move	Controller Command
Double Fist Drop	move into turnbuckle + ▼

THROW GROGGY OPPONENT INTO TURNBUCKLE

Name of Move	Controller Command
Corner Crunch	Tap Ⓐ + Ⓐ
Macho Man Drop	Hold Ⓐ + Ⓐ
Super DDT	Hold Ⓐ + ⇑ + Ⓐ

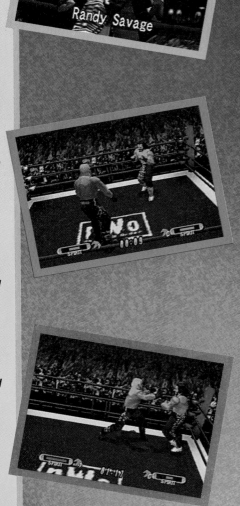

Randy Savage

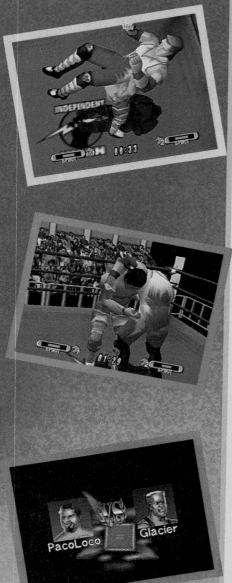

GLACIER

Height: 6' 2"
Weight: 250 lbs.
Signature Move: Cryonic Kick

Profile

Glacier is the top student in the combative form of fighting that combines martial arts with wrestling, and is the Chosen One to pass on his knowledge to WCW fans and wrestlers alike. Glacier's Cryonic Kick finisher, a kick off the top rope, is unlike anything in the sport. Glacier places his ceremonial Samurai warrior's helmet on a ring-post during matches so he can keep it under his watchful eye.

Punching and Kicking Moves

Name of Move	Controller Command
Karate Chop	Tap Ⓑ close
Karate Kick	Tap Ⓑ far
Karate Punch	⇑ + Tap Ⓑ close
Side Kick	⇑ + Tap Ⓑ far
Standing Drop Kick	Hold Ⓑ
Spin Kick	⇑ + Hold Ⓑ

Front Grapples—Weak

Name of Move	Controller Command
Super Chop	Tap Ⓐ + Ⓐ
Fireman's Carry	Tap Ⓐ + ⇑ + Ⓐ
Glacier Tackle	Tap Ⓐ + ⇓ + Ⓐ
Elbow Smash	Tap Ⓐ + Ⓑ
Tundra Suplex	Tap Ⓐ + ⇑ + Ⓑ
Pile Driver	Tap Ⓐ + ⇓ + Ⓑ

Rear Grapples—Weak

Name of Move	Controller Command
Twist Back Drop	Tap Ⓐ + Ⓐ
Knee Breaker	Tap Ⓐ + Ⓑ

Front Grapples—Strong

Name of Move	Controller Command
Neck Breaker	Hold Ⓐ + Ⓐ
Top Rope Clothesline Slam	Hold Ⓐ + ⇑ + Ⓐ
Backslide	Hold Ⓐ + ⇓ + Ⓐ
Belly to Back Suplex	Hold Ⓐ + Ⓑ
Blizzard Takedown	Hold Ⓐ + ⇑ + Ⓑ
Northern Light Suplex	Hold Ⓐ + ⇓ + Ⓑ

Rear Grapples—Strong

Name of Move	Controller Command
Body Rack	Hold Ⓐ + Ⓐ
German Suplex	Hold Ⓐ + Ⓑ

Whip to Ropes

Name of Move	Controller Command
Arm-Drag Takedown	Hold Ⓐ + D Pad toward ropes + ▼ + Tap Ⓐ
Leg Scissor Sweep	Hold Ⓐ + D Pad toward ropes + ▼ + ⇑ + Tap Ⓐ
High Backflip	Hold Ⓐ + D Pad toward ropes + ▼ + Hold Ⓐ
Arm Bar Takedown	Hold Ⓐ + D Pad toward ropes + ▼ + ⇑ + Hold Ⓐ

Special Attacks (When Spirit Meter Is Flashing)

FROM THE FRONT

Name of Move	Controller Command
Cryonic Kick	Hold ▼ + Analog Stick

FROM THE REAR

Name of Move	Controller Command
Full Nelson Suplex	Hold Ⓐ + Analog Stick

Opponent on Mat

FACE UP

Name of Move	Controller Command
Side Headlock	move near head, Tap Ⓐ
Boston Crab	move near legs, Tap Ⓐ
Elbow Drop	Tap Ⓑ

FACE DOWN

Name of Move	Controller Command
Camel Clutch	move near head, Tap Ⓐ
Crucifix Crunch	move near legs, Tap Ⓐ
Knee Smash	Tap Ⓑ

Rope and Turnbuckle Moves

OPPONENT ON MAT

Name of Move	Controller Command
Flying Knee	move into turnbuckle + ▼

OPPONENT STANDING

Name of Move	Controller Command
Flying Kick	move into turnbuckle + ▼

THROW GROGGY OPPONENT INTO TURNBUCKLE

Name of Move	Controller Command
Riding Punch	Tap Ⓐ + Ⓐ
Glacier Suplex	Hold Ⓐ + Ⓐ
Blizzard Bomb	Hold Ⓐ + ⇑ + Ⓐ

Glacier

IU Single Champion

Grand championship title match

WRATH

Height: 6' 8"
Weight: 295 lbs.
Signature Move: Death Penalty

Profile

Expect to pay dearly for your crimes when you step into the ring with Wrath, appropriately named. Don't even bother pleading for mercy, because this 6' 8" powerhouse believes in capital punishment. Opponents cower when they see him enter the ring cloaked in his armor.

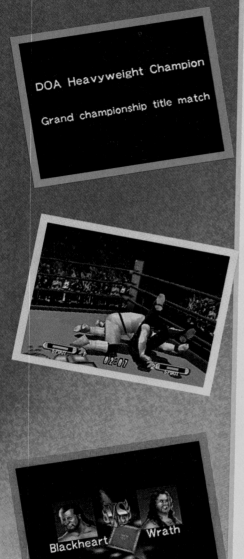

DOA Heavyweight Champion

Grand championship title match

Blackheart   Wrath

Punching and Kicking Moves

Name of Move	Controller Command
Pain Punch	Tap Ⓑ close
Knee Kick	Tap Ⓑ far
Slicing Chop	⇑ + Tap Ⓑ close
Knee Kick	⇑ + Tap Ⓑ far
Drop Kick	Hold Ⓑ
Forearm Clothesline	⇑ + Hold Ⓑ

Front Grapples—Weak

Name of Move	Controller Command
Forearm Smash	Tap Ⓐ + Ⓐ
Coconut Crush	Tap Ⓐ + ⇑ + Ⓐ
Body Slam	Tap Ⓐ + ⇓ + Ⓐ
Neck Breaker	Tap Ⓐ + Ⓑ
Press Slam	Tap Ⓐ + ⇑ + Ⓑ
Pile Driver	Tap Ⓐ + ⇓ + Ⓑ

Rear Grapples—Weak

Name of Move	Controller Command
Spine Buster	Tap Ⓐ + Ⓐ
Atomic Drop	Tap Ⓐ + Ⓑ

Front Grapples—Strong

Name of Move	Controller Command
Belly to Back Suplex	Hold Ⓐ + Ⓐ
Vertical Suplex	Hold Ⓐ + ⇑ + Ⓐ
Shoulder Breaker	Hold Ⓐ + ⇓ + Ⓐ
Side Buster	Hold Ⓐ + Ⓑ
Canadian Back Breaker	Hold Ⓐ + ⇑ + Ⓑ
Power Bomb Press	Hold Ⓐ + ⇓ + Ⓑ

Rear Grapples—Strong

Name of Move	Controller Command
Blindside Bash	Hold Ⓐ + Ⓐ
Painbomb	Hold Ⓐ + Ⓑ

Whip to Ropes

Name of Move	Controller Command
Arm-Drag Takedown	Hold Ⓐ + D Pad toward ropes + ▼ + Tap Ⓐ
Carry Over Slam	Hold Ⓐ + D Pad toward ropes + ▼ + ⇑ + Tap Ⓐ
Power Slam	Hold Ⓐ + D Pad toward ropes + ▼ + Hold Ⓐ
Power Lift Body Slam	Hold Ⓐ + D Pad toward ropes + ▼ + ⇑ + Hold Ⓐ

Special Attacks (When Spirit Meter Is Flashing)

FROM THE FRONT

Name of Move	Controller Command
Death Penalty	Hold Ⓐ + Analog Stick

FROM THE REAR

Name of Move	Controller Command
Grapple Doctor Bomb	Hold Ⓐ + Analog Stick

Opponent on Mat

FACE UP

Name of Move	Controller Command
Side Headlock	move near head, Tap Ⓐ
Boston Crab	move near legs, Tap Ⓐ
Falling Punch	Tap Ⓑ

FACE DOWN

Name of Move	Controller Command
Camel Clutch	move near head, Tap Ⓐ
Leg Lock	move near legs, Tap Ⓐ
Elbow Drop	Tap Ⓑ

Rope and Turnbuckle Moves

OPPONENT ON MAT

Name of Move	Controller Command
Flying Knee	move into turnbuckle + ▼

OPPONENT STANDING

Name of Move	Controller Command
Top Rope Clothesline	move into turnbuckle + ▼

THROW GROGGY OPPONENT INTO TURNBUCKLE

Name of Move	Controller Command
Cross Arm Punch	Tap Ⓐ + Ⓐ
Brain Buster	Hold Ⓐ + Ⓐ
Riding Punch	Hold Ⓐ + ⇑ + Ⓐ

World Cruiserweight Champion

Grand championship title match

BLACK WIDOW

Height: 5' 9"
Weight: 194 lbs.
Signature Moves: Spinning Head Sickle,
Death Coil

Profile

Heiress to a fabulous fortune and the only survivor of a horrible north sea yachting disaster that killed her family, little else is known about the mysterious and reserved Black Widow. Resistant to human interaction, Black Widow's only love now is money. Most professional wrestlers agree that the world would never see the forceful Black Widow appear in public were it not for the fact that every booker on the planet would pay any amount to coerce the Black Widow to appear on their cards. There isn't a pro wrestler on Earth that fancies a kiss from this spider woman!

Punching and Kicking Moves

Name of Move	Controller Command
Slap	Tap Ⓑ close
Low Kick	Tap Ⓑ far
Punch	⇑ + Tap Ⓑ close
Spin Kick	⇑ + Tap Ⓑ far
High Kick	Hold Ⓑ
Drop Kick	⇑ + Hold Ⓑ

Front Grapples—Weak

Name of Move	Controller Command
Uppercut Punch	Tap Ⓐ + Ⓐ
Fireman's Carry	Tap Ⓐ + ⇑ + Ⓐ
Body Slam	Tap Ⓐ + ⇓ + Ⓐ
Twisting Elbow	Tap Ⓐ + Ⓑ
Snap Suplex	Tap Ⓐ + ⇑ + Ⓑ
Pile Driver	Tap Ⓐ + ⇓ + Ⓑ

Rear Grapples—Weak

Name of Move	Controller Command
Widow Crush	Tap Ⓐ + Ⓐ
Backdrop Slam	Tap Ⓐ + Ⓑ

Front Grapples—Strong

Name of Move	Controller Command
Widow's Peak	Hold Ⓐ + Ⓐ
Spider Slam	Hold Ⓐ + ⇑ + Ⓐ
Knee Slam Press	Hold Ⓐ + ⇓ + Ⓐ
Suplex Sting	Hold Ⓐ + Ⓑ
Crucifix Slam	Hold Ⓐ + ⇑ + Ⓑ
Widow-Maker	Hold Ⓐ + ⇓ + Ⓑ

Rear Grapples—Strong

Name of Move	Controller Command
Shoulder Spin Press	Hold Ⓐ + Ⓐ
Spider-Web Slam	Hold Ⓐ + Ⓑ

Whip to Ropes

Name of Move	Controller Command
Leg Scissors Sweep	Hold Ⓐ + D Pad toward ropes + ▼ + Tap Ⓐ
Shoulder Flip	Hold Ⓐ + D Pad toward ropes + ▼ + ⇑ + Tap Ⓐ
Spinning Backbreaker	Hold Ⓐ + D Pad toward ropes + ▼ + Hold Ⓐ
Spinning Head Sickle	Hold Ⓐ + D Pad toward ropes + ▼ + ⇑ + Hold Ⓐ

Special Attacks (When Spirit Meter Is Flashing)

FROM THE FRONT

Name of Move	Controller Command
Death Coil	Hold Ⓐ + Analog Stick

FROM THE REAR

Name of Move	Controller Command
Widow's Press	Hold Ⓐ + Analog Stick

Opponent on Mat

FACE UP

Name of Move	Controller Command
Face Lock	move near head, Tap Ⓐ
Stomach Pump	move near legs, Tap Ⓐ
Somersault Splash	Tap Ⓑ

FACE DOWN

Name of Move	Controller Command
Spider Clutch	move near head, Tap Ⓐ
Reverse Clutch	move near legs, Tap Ⓐ
Leg Drop	Tap Ⓑ

Rope and Turnbuckle Moves

OPPONENT ON MAT

Name of Move	Controller Command
Flying Knee	move into turnbuckle + ▼
Spider Splash	move into turnbuckle + ▼

OPPONENT STANDING

Name of Move	Controller Command
Widow Kick	move into turnbuckle + ▼

MOONSAULT

Name of Move	Controller Command
Web Walk	run toward ropes, ⇑ + Ⓐ

THROW GROGGY OPPONENT INTO TURNBUCKLE

Name of Move	Controller Command
Corner Rumble	Tap Ⓐ + Ⓐ
Turnbuckle Tradeoff	Tap Ⓐ + Ⓑ
Venom DDT	Hold Ⓐ + Ⓐ
Widow's Sting	Hold Ⓐ + ⇑ + Ⓐ

JOE BRUISER

World Heavyweight Champion
Grand championship title match

Height: 6' 7"
Weight: 275 lbs.
Signature Move: Big Right Uppercut to the Chin

Profile

Free-wheelin' and tough-talkin', Joe Bruiser is the living embodiment of the irresistible force. Joe Bruiser's father, Alexander Augustus Bruiser, recognized that even as a young man growing up in the steel belt of Pennsylvania, Joe could be one the world's greatest boxers. Alexander dedicated his life to providing Joe with the discipline he needed to achieve that greatness. Now, independently wealthy from his pro boxing career, Joe fights in the pro wrestling organizations just to please his many young fans.

Defensive Moves

Name of Move	Controller Command
Guard and Counter	Ⓡ
Duck	Ⓛ

Offensive Moves (from the Front)

Name of Move	Controller Command
Right Cross	Tap Ⓑ
Left Jab	⇑ + Tab
Left Uppercut to the Midsection	Hold Ⓑ
Right Uppercut to the Chin	⇑ + Hold Ⓑ
Right Cross	Tap Ⓐ
Left Cross	⇑ + Tap Ⓐ
Head Butt	Hold Ⓐ
Big Right Uppercut to the Chin	⇑ + Hold Ⓐ

Offensive Moves (from the Rear)

Name of Move	Controller Command
Kidney Punch	Tap Ⓐ
Right Uppercut to Kidneys	Hold Ⓐ
Rabbit Punch	Tap Ⓑ
1–2 Combo— Right to Head, Left to Kidneys	Hold Ⓑ

Opponent on Mat (Face Up)

Name of Move	Controller Command
Knee Smash	Tap Ⓑ

Opponent on Mat (Face Down)

Name of Move	Controller Command
Kick	Tap Ⓑ

Other Moves

Name of Move	Controller Command
Forward Front Kick	D Pad toward ropes + ▼ + Ⓑ
Climb Turnbuckle and Appeal to Crowd	D Pad toward turnbuckle + ▼
Pin	▼

too much for you?

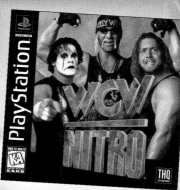

GameShark™
This is not a game.
It's a game enhancer.
Plug it in
and turn it on.
Reveal the hidden.
Unleash the fury.
Feed on weakness.
Never lose
and never die.
Abuse the Power.
INTERACT
GAME PRODUCTS
Obtain the latest codes from: www.gameshark.com • 1.900.773.SHARK (Call costs $1.29/minute. You must be 18 years of age or have parent's permission to call.) • Dangerous Waters Newsletter (For more info call 410.238.2424) • Gaming Mags • GameShark available for PlayStation™, Sega Saturn™ and Nintendo®64. ©1997 InterAct Accessories, Inc. InterAct is a trademark of STD Manufacturing Ltd. PlayStation is a trademark of Sony Computer Entertainment Company of America. Saturn is a trademark of Sega Enterprises Ltd. Nintendo 64 is a trademark of Nintendo of America Inc.

to order, call prima at
1-800-531-2343